Queen Esther's Reflection

A PORTRAIT OF GRACE, COURAGE, AND EXCELLENCE

Ann Platz

Ann Platz loves Paula

NEW HOPE
PUBLISHERS

Birmingham, Alabama

New Hope® Publishers
P. O. Box 12065
Birmingham, AL 35202-2065
www.newhopepublishers.com
New Hope Publishers is a division of WMU®.
© 2007 by Ann Platz
All rights reserved. First printing 2007.
Printed in the United States of America.

Library of Congress Cataloging-in-Publication Data

Platz, Ann.
  Queen Esther's reflection : a portrait of grace, courage, and excellence / Ann Platz.
      p. cm.
  ISBN 978-1-59669-012-7 (sc)
  1. Esther, Queen of Persia. 2. Christian women—Religious life. I. Title.
BS580.E8P53 2007
222'.9092—dc22

                                                      2007009875

ISBN -10: 1-59669-012-7
ISBN-13: 978-1-59669-012-7
N064144 • 0409 • 2M2

Dedication
This book
is dedicated

to my beloved husband
John Oliver Platz, my Mordecai,
whose love, protection, guidance, and godliness
have influenced me greatly.

And in
memory of my father
Senator Marshall Burns Williams,
my first Mordecai and mentor.

Thank you both for all that
you imparted into my life.

"*I have set watchmen on your walls, O Jerusalem;*
They shall never hold their peace day or night.
You who make mention of the Lord, do not keep silent.
And give Him no rest till He establishes
And till He makes Jerusalem a praise in the earth."

—Isaiah 62:6–7

Contents

Introduction

Since early in my childhood, I have been captivated by the story of Queen Esther of Persia, one of the great women of the Bible. I believe many women find her intriguing and fascinating. Not only was she a courageous heroine, one worth emulating, she was winner of the greatest beauty pageant of her time, married to the most powerful king in the land, and giver of the greatest dinner parties in the Bible! Her story is filled with the stuff of romance novels, and like most women, I love romance.

Her story is also very much connected to our lives as women today. Even though she is a long-ago queen, I can learn from her. I can relate to her. Her story is about a woman's desire to be as beautiful as she can be. I can relate to that. As a young girl, I was fascinated with creams, lotions, fingernail polish, silver combs and brushes, and all things feminine. I loved perfume, powders, and jewelry. My afternoons were spent playing dress-up. Like most little girls, I pretended to be a princess bride—veil and all!

Esther's story is also about hospitality. I can relate to that. As I grew into young womanhood, my natural inclination was to pay attention to colors, fabrics, furnishings, and things that pertained to the beauty of the home. Studying interior design magazines occupied hours of my time. This led to my study of interior design. I have dedicated more than 30 years of my life to a career in making homes beautiful. My design company, Ann Platz & Co., has been the fulfillment of the desires of my childhood. With each client, I listen, and then try to interpret their special dream. Understanding the role that beauty and design play in our lives, I seek to make every home a palace.

Esther's story is also about manners and protocol. Growing up in a southern world of hospitality, I was taught the importance of social graces. My father served in the South Carolina State Senate for almost 50 years. Because my family was involved in politics, we often entertained guests in our spacious country home, named Willbrook, in the Low Country of South Carolina. My parents lived in a political world where protocol, manners, and etiquette were expected to be a part of our lives.

My mother, "Miss Margaret," is well known as one of the most gracious hostesses in the South. I would often sit at her feet and watch her practice her beauty routines as she dressed for special social events. Much to my delight, Mother dressed in beaded ball gowns and glittering accessories. It was easy for me to love the biblical heroine, Esther. She reminded me of my mother. Growing up in South, you learn—beauty matters! Its secrets are passed down from one generation to the next.

As a child in my Sunday School classes, I loved hearing about Esther. I listened as my teacher told of Esther's life as an orphan destined to be a queen. I was swept away with the image of a queen-in-the-making and the danger that lurked in the palace. As a mature woman, I have read the Book of Esther many times, gleaning much about what it means to be a woman with a mission.

My love of people, design, and beauty has led me to host dinner parties as I saw my mother do. I have often entertained at formal dinner affairs, but nothing to compare with the legendary Esther. Her private parties were planned with fabulous food, great beauty, and much purpose. I can picture her dinner party with Haman and the king—everything planned to perfection.

Esther received brilliant mentoring from her cousin and protector, Mordecai. Over the years, I have seen the need to mentor many women. I am able to do this because of the incredible mentoring that I have received. Several dynamic women poured blessings and graces into my life. I am forever thankful for their impartation to me.

Mentoring is a part of my spiritual calling. These women are my *spiritual daughters*. As I attempt to inspire them to know more about God, I always ask that they first read the Book of Esther. I want them to see a life submitted to the Lord and one that depended on a one-on-one mentoring partnership. I start my mentoring program with principles from the life of Esther. I help women today learn how to be godly women who are also successful in these same areas: marriage, purpose, refinement, submission, loyalty, and courage. Because Esther yielded to her mentor-cousin Mordecai, he was able to lead, guide, and prepare Esther for her destiny. There are many life lessons from Esther's story.

In *Queen Esther's Reflection*, I set out to unveil the mysterious Esther. This woman, whose physical beauty outshone all others, was called by God and put in place as a queen for a purpose—the deliverance of God's chosen people, the Jews, from annihilation. The shining words of Scripture from the Book of Esther, "*Who knows whether you have come to the kingdom for such a time as this?*" speak volumes to women today. Her courage and her willingness to lay down her life for her people, reminds me of my Savior, Jesus Christ, who would lay down His own life to provide a means for all people everywhere to be saved from eternal death.

After researching the life of this great beauty, this holy woman, and having written what I believed was the final chapter of this book, I paused to reflect on all that God has given me for you—and to catch my breath. What I caught, however, was the breath of God! As is often the case with my writing, revelation has continued when I feel as if the last word has been written. The message of this book is one that I had only partly grasped in the two-plus years of prayerful work on the manuscript. What you are now holding in your hands is the revised version—God's way.

The overriding story of this one woman's heroic life reveals many things:

- God has a strategic plan for your life.
- God has a network of people to surround you.
- God has a "*for such a time as this*" for each of us.
- God will give you favor.
- God partners with those who answer His call.

Today, as a wife, mother, grandmother, and even as a great-grandmother, I want to impart God's grace and courage to the people I love. I consider the love I have for my own two daughters and their children and all the spiritual daughters God has so graciously given me. I think of the legacy of truth—the precious and the practical—that I want to leave behind when I am no longer with them. It's everything I ever wanted them to know about God's eternal truths, an end-time message of all that He loves and cherishes most. This book is written for them and for you.

—Ann Platz

Esther

Gracious Father, we thank You for giving to the world Esther of Persia. Dear Lord, do not allow her to remain a mystery to us. Let us behold what You created in her that is meant to challenge and convict. Give us the fragrance of who she is—Your Esther. Let us read her diary. Let us know her as You have known her. Allow her to step off the pages of Holy Scripture and reveal herself to the body of Christ. Give us Esther revelation.

Take this book around the world. Deposit and distribute it where it needs to go. Give us a fresh anointing. Give us fresh manna. Blow life into this manuscript. Breathe Esther's mystique into each woman who reads these words, and allow her spiritual beauty to come forth.

In the precious name of Jesus, we pray. Amen.

Part One

Queen Esther's Story

"The fruit of the Spirit is love, joy, peace, longsuffering, kind-ness, goodness, faithfulness, gentleness, self control. . . . If we live in the Spirit, let us also walk in the Spirit."
—Galatians 5:22–23, 25

CHAPTER 1

Woman of Grace

Glimpses of Grace
*"You have found grace in My sight, and I know you
by name."*
—Exodus 33:17

Y OU WOULD recognize her anywhere. She enters the
room with an air of quiet confidence. She does not
come in like a storm; rather, like a gentle breeze. Instantly
you will sense that here is a seasoned woman of prayer, a
veteran of many spiritual battles, and a woman whose life
is a reflection of the Master's heart. There is a balanced harmony between her spirit and His, a deep integrity refined
in the fires of life. She has no arrogance, no haughty, lime-
light-seeking, take-charge attitude, only humility and the
essence of servanthood. Everything about her speaks of love
and graciousness. She has been disciplined through proper
protocol. She is a student of the social graces. She is that
"woman of grace," the woman you and I can become. Her
name is Esther, queen of Persia.

The Bible story found in the Book of Esther is fascinating—a tale with all the mystery of a modern-day drama, complete with deception, palace intrigue, and a murderous plot! Even more compelling is Esther herself. This mysterious beauty appears from obscurity and captures the heart of the most powerful man on earth, the pagan king of Persia. Her attributes of grace and godliness eclipse even her outer beauty and gain her the king's respect. Their subsequent marriage positions her strategically to fulfill her destiny—to step into place on the world stage and end a horrible scheme to annihilate her people, the Jews. Esther was chosen . . . *"for such a time as this."*

You probably already know the story. It's a classic. Esther—beauty queen, expatriate queen, covert queen, servant queen. From my earliest memories of great women of the Bible—from childhood Sunday School days—I have been captivated by the legendary Esther of Persia. Initially, the yearlong preparations required for Esther's presentation to the king appealed to my budding designer instincts—specifically to my desire for transformation, beauty, order, form, and color. The lovely fragrances used in the regimens and her special tutoring in the social graces added their own appeal.

But the story held deeper meanings as well. Esther was shimmering like an undiscovered treasure, a diamond, or rare pearl. Some facets of this precious jewel, this many-splendored story of mystery, romance, and palace politics, may only be perceived by the spiritual eye. From the beginning, we can see that this woman's physical beauty was merely a device used by God to achieve His sovereign purposes—the deliverance of the Jews from certain death. You might also recognize, along with countless others, that she was a type of "savior," foreshadowing the time when Jesus Christ would lay down His own life to provide a means for all people everywhere to be saved from eternal death.

As an orphaned Jewish girl living in captivity, it was Esther's divine destiny to act as an ambassador of the kingdom of heaven at a critical time in the history of Israel. In the process, of course, the beautiful captive became the conqueror and married the king. Only God could have conceived such a plot! Queen Esther's remarkable life set her apart from all the other women of her day—her absolute obedience, her physical beauty matched only by her spiritual beauty, her fierce loyalty to the God of her fathers, her daring encounter with the king at risk to her own life.

But does this story have any real connection to our lives as women today? Is it just as unrealistic as last year's bodice-ripper novel, thrown in a dusty corner? Does Esther live and breathe with a message for real women of today? Is there anything we can learn from this portrait of a long-ago queen? Esther's story is not just something to be dusted off once a year. It's not just a strange tale of an ancient king's unconventional search for a queen. The story of Esther holds truths about spiritual beauty that are vital and enriching for Christian women today. Want to know Esther's true beauty secrets? Read on!

Spiritually Beautiful

Becoming a true woman of grace on mission for God should be the ultimate goal of every contemporary Christian woman. As a spiritually beautiful woman in every situation and in every season, you:

*   Are called for a specific purpose in God's design.
*   Will allow the Holy Spirit to prepare you.
*   Come under authority—both natural and spiritual.
*   Receive correction and instruction with humility.
*   Become a woman of prayer and fasting.
*   Allow God to promote you.
*   Understand the timing of the Lord.
*   Make friends easily and know how to keep them.
*   Mentor others with your wise counsel.

In Esther's era, as well as in ours, these are not only the ingredients of gracious living—a style of life that transcends mere protocol and party manners—it is the beginning of *kingdom living*. When you move into the realm of spiritual maturity and abundance, when you see your surroundings and circumstances as opportunities to be used by God for kingdom purposes, everything changes!

Esther is a portrait of grace and beauty, incredible courage, and true excellence—a role model for the twenty-first-century woman. Let me begin by telling you her story, found in the Bible's Book of Esther.

Persia, Fifth Century B.C.

The chronicle of Esther reads almost like a classic movie script, telling of dramatic events that occurred when the Jews were captives in Persia. The leading man was King Ahasuerus (called Xerxes in some Bible translations). The story of his most favored wife, Esther, was set against the contrasting backdrop of splendor and poverty, freedom and bondage, great good and great evil—with Esther and her people held captive in the heart of a pagan empire.

Centuries before Jesus was born, Ahasuerus ruled the Persian Empire, which consisted of 127 provinces, from India to Ethiopia. King Ahasuerus ruled from his massive palace complex in the capital city of Susa. In the third year of his reign, the king called for a celebration, to which he invited all of his ministers and governors of the provinces. For six months Ahasuerus put on an elaborate exhibition to display "*the riches of his glorious kingdom and the splendor of his excellent majesty*" (Esther 1:4). He entertained lavishly with the finest food and drink, music and dance. At the close of this season, King Ahasuerus held a seven-day feast in the court of the gardens of the summer palace.

I love parties, and there is nothing I enjoy more than entertaining 50 or 75 of my "closest friends," but the king's party was a major national event. The guest list was the entire population of the town!

As I read the account in the "society column" of the first chapter of Esther, I realized that I could have been the decorator for this affair. The king's designer used all my favorite colors and fabrics: "*White and blue linen curtains fastened with cords of fine linen and purple on silver rods and marble pillars; and the couches were of gold and silver on a mosaic pavement of alabaster, turquoise, and white and black marble. And they served drinks in golden vessels, each vessel being different from the other*" (Esther 1:6–7). Don't you love it? What a visual feast!

Wine was flowing freely at this party, and the king had given orders that everyone was to drink as much as they wanted. The king was apparently drinking a good bit himself, for Esther 1:10 tells us that on day seven of the party, "*the heart of the king was merry with wine.*"

Vashti, the Villainess

Meanwhile, Queen Vashti, his wife, was having her own little get-together as she hosted the prominent women from the palace. One would imagine that this was quite a different scene from the king's drunken soirée.

On day seven, just as she was serving the hors d'oeuvres, she received a royal summons from the king, delivered by special courier. She was to appear in his court, "*wearing her royal crown, in order to show her beauty to the people and the officials, for she was beautiful to behold*" (Esther 1:11).

Not only was the queen astonishingly beautiful, but she had impeccable credentials—royal blood. As one reference cites: "Her grandfather was Nebuchadnezzar, who had destroyed Solomon's Temple in Jerusalem and drove the Jews into exile and her father was Belshazzar, the last in a line of great Babylonian kings, whose dramatic death is described in the Book of Daniel." A person would think Queen Vashti had it all—beauty, a great bloodline, co-regency of the richest kingdom in the then-known world, anything her heart could desire. But when the time came to prove herself, she made one fatal mistake—she chose not to submit to authority. She rebelled.

In Vashti's defense, the king's command does seem to be unusual, or at the very least untimely. Was she supposed to abandon her guests and parade herself before her husband and his drunken friends? What modern woman would put up with that? "I have every right to refuse," she might say. "He's been drunk for months. And just look at those men he hangs out with. They're behaving like animals!" In our minds she may have been justified to protest, but in her day, to refuse the king's command was suicide.

Granted, some marriages today can be just as volatile and life-threatening as Vashti's. Does God insist on absolute obedience to one's marriage vows under any and all circumstances? We'll search the Word for the answer to that question and others in another chapter.

Vashti's choice was costly for her. After consultation with his wise men, the king deposed her as an example to all married women in the land. She lost her royal position and was never again brought to the king. He and his advisors intended to nip such marital rebellion in the bud.

Nothing more is heard of Vashti. But the world now knows all about her replacement—the beauty with a mysterious past.

Esther, "Star" of Persia

Esther is found in only one book of the Bible, but her story, cloaked in a tale of palace intrigue, is one of the most powerful portrayals of a daring woman ever recorded.

Esther's Persian name, meaning "star," was prophetic in that she would rise from obscurity to brighten the darkness of the pagan world in which she was a captive. Interestingly the history of her family line is linked with that of Vashti's. Generations ago, Vashti's grandfather had sacked the capital city of Israel and carried off Esther's forefathers. Esther was born during this captivity, positioned by God to reverse history and bring His promised redemption to His people. He had blessed her with natural beauty, but it was her heart and spirit that shone brightest from her lovely face. From the beginning, God knew the plans He had for her and He protected and provided nurture for her until she was ready to step into her role.

Esther's Hebrew name, Hadassah, means "myrtle." The myrtle of Old Testament days was an evergreen tree with dark, glossy leaves and fragrant white flowers. This tree, with its leaves, flowers, and berries, was used in perfume and in seasoning food. Like the evergreen, Esther's faith and hope would flourish through all the seasons of her life and her fragrant aroma would linger down through the centuries.

But she would need much preparation and tender care before she faced her future. That responsibility would fall to a man named Mordecai. After Esther's father and mother died, her cousin Mordecai took her in and brought her up as his own daughter. Mordecai was a descendant of the tribe of Benjamin, the younger brother of Joseph, son of Jacob.

Mordecai would tutor and train Esther in the ways of God, keeping her faith strong in that foreign culture. Mordecai would be her mentor during her reign as queen, when she interceded for their people; and it was he who would prompt her lines, her entrances, and her exits in a drama entitled "For Such a Time as This."

The king's advisors convinced him to gather beautiful young virgins from all the provinces and choose a new queen from among them. Esther was brought to the palace as part of this gathering. Challenged to become a contestant in a national beauty quest to find the next queen of Persia,

Esther had her work cut out for her. The king of Persia was one of the most powerful men in the world, an unbeliever, an enemy of Esther's native country, and a man who had many women in his harem.

From the time she entered the palace, Esther was a favorite of Hegai, the eunuch who served as custodian of the women. Only eunuchs were allowed access to the women in the harem, in order to preserve their sexual exclusivity for the king. Hegai saw that Esther stayed in the best place in the house of women, had the best maidservants, and received extra beauty treatments, and knew just what the king liked. Every one of the virgins in the harem went through 12 months of beauty treatments. After her time of preparation, she went in to the king. Every girl went in a virgin and came out a concubine—every girl except the one who would come out a queen. And all this time, Esther never let anyone know that she was a Jew—a member of a captive race. Also, all this time, her cousin Mordecai kept careful watch nearby, always asking about her welfare.

No one can dispute that Esther was the object of a shallow search for a wife by today's standards. The king was powerful, controlling, spoiled, and harsh—terrible husband material! But we know the end of the story. Not only does Esther win the beauty contest, she finds such incredible favor with King Ahasuerus that at the appointed time, as his queen, she asks the unimaginable—freedom for the Jewish people.

The marriage worked. It did more than that. It was a raging success! What was Esther's secret? I want to know, don't you? This is one biblical heroine we need to study. Esther has much to teach today's Christian woman, especially how to succeed at your marriage while fulfilling the call of God on your life.

For Such a Time as This

Do you know that you also were put in place "*for such a time as this*"? God's grace has no time limits but God does have a very definite timeline. He has a plan for the work that must be done in each of us. This may sound strange to you, but your life did not begin at birth or even at conception. You were preconceived in the heart of God (see Jeremiah 1:5). He knew you. He chose you. He purposed you. He set you apart. He plotted the length of your earthly existence, even to the number of days you would live (see Psalm 139:13, 15–16). He knows the number of hairs on your head, whether blonde, brunette, auburn, or snow white (see Matthew 10:30). God knew, too, the choices you would make and how those choices would affect His overall plan.

From the very beginning of time, in the infancy of creation, God was thinking of a way out—for when the man and woman He had created to live in the Garden happened to fall from their happy state of grace. God's merciful provision was the ultimate gift to mankind—a redeemer—His only Son. He also activated the rescue squad of intercessors and prophets who would intercede for you and prophesy over you through the ages. Some prayer warriors took up the cause long before you were born; wise great-great-grandmothers and grandfathers with the vision to see the unseen and to pray for generations yet to come.

Even before God graciously manifested His love for all mankind by sending Jesus into the world, He was at work bestowing His grace, or special favor, on men and women who rose up to play pivotal roles in His ultimate plan. Joseph, a prisoner in Egypt for 13 long years, was promoted to second-in-command under the powerful Egyptian pharaoh, to save God's people from death by famine. David, a man after God's own heart and an obscure shepherd from the hills of Judea, was crowned king of Israel, to save the kingdom for God's purposes.

Esther, the orphaned Jewess living in Babylonian captivity far from her homeland, was raised up to win a national contest and be selected from hundreds of women to become queen of Persia, to save God's people from annihilation. Each of these biblical models was a "savior," pointing to the one true Savior of the world, God's own Son, who would break into human history in a future century.

How interesting, too, that each of these "saviors" endured some kind of confinement. In Joseph's case, it was an actual prison with bars. David was confined by the circumstances of youth and politics; Esther was confined to a harem. Yet God used them anyway, just as He can use you and me! He set each of them free to fulfill His purpose and to reveal their own unique destiny. Still, if they had not heard the call and submitted to it, laying down their own agendas, they would have forfeited the opportunity of a lifetime to impact God's kingdom for all eternity.

We may choose to live out the role assigned to us by the divine casting director, or we may choose to write our own script—and suffer the consequences.

Stepping into the Light

Some people choose to live close to the edge, in disobedience and rebellion. Sin is dangerous, deep, and dark. It lures subtly, with the promise of easy installment payments. There is the innocent flirtation, the questionable amusement, the compromising companion that leads to trouble. The first time, you may stumble into an affair or some other kind of sin, with no intention of staying there. A prick of conscience serves as a warning signal. But before long, the sin becomes familiar and even friendly. Finally, there is no turning back, and you are locked into a habit that slowly destroys all hope.

There comes a moment in time, or perhaps many moments in His great mercy, when Jesus will call, saying, "Follow Me." You have a choice to remain in the kingdom of darkness and all that this world holds, or to be rescued and step into the kingdom of light. It is a decision each person will have to make. A kingdom transfer occurs when you choose Jesus. From the moment of accepting Him as Savior, it is all about a new way of living—gracious living, kingdom living, covenant living.

Eternal life is God's promise, sealed by the blood of Jesus. God is the original promise keeper. His invitation is not limited to a privileged few, since He is *not willing that any should perish but that all should come to repentance* (2 Peter 3:9). Kingdom living is God's open-door policy to all.

Esther lived in Old Testament times, before Jesus had come. But she represents His Spirit of sacrifice through her willingness to lay down her life for her people. Although Esther may have understood only a little of her true purpose in life, God was working behind the scenes. You can learn to recognize your purpose through prayer, through digging deep into the His Word, and through listening to the wisdom of godly mentors.

God's plan for you is to do mighty things for Him in His kingdom. This requires all of the disciplines that Esther practiced: purifying the physical body; cleansing the soul—mind, will, and emotions; and nurturing your spiritual being, that part of you that will live forever. Be patient. This total makeover will take a lifetime.

A Face in the Crowd

What did this young woman possess that so moved the heart of a pagan king that he made her his queen? It was much more than a pretty face—it had something to do with being different, exotic, and rare. When someone beautiful and exquisite from another country is amongst you, you sense a beauty that is from the kingdom of God. He has filled the world with exotic people, different races, and the rare and precious. This loveliness moves beyond beauty—the essence is something spiritual.

With my children safely in my parents' care and my interior design business on hold for the holidays, I once treated myself to a post-Christmas present with a dear friend—a week at one of the South's most prestigious health and beauty retreats. Not being a vain woman, my objective was to relax and enjoy time away from an exhausting work schedule and the duties that surrounded being the single parent of two young, energetic daughters. My friend had persuaded me that this idyllic seaside spot was the place to do it.

Never having had a spa experience, this was heavenly; truly a whole new world for me. I adored the pampering. Some of the lotions and creams the attendants used on our skin reminded me of my Grandmother Winnie, a family beauty and one of my first mentors. It was she who introduced me to the joys of mixing potions of crushed strawberries and cold cream to slather on our faces when I went for visits to her home in Charleston as a small child.

The spa facials we were now enjoying were no homemade remedy. Expertly applied, we received a different mask each day for seven days—strawberry, cucumber, lavender, and all combinations of delightful herbal concoctions. Seven facials! Being the practical type, I would never have paid such a price if they had not been part of the package deal. In fact, I would have thought that one facial was sufficient.

At the end of the week, however, when I examined my face with a magnifying glass, I found that my skin was flawless; as soft and smooth as a baby's! It had taken seven treatments to slough off the dead cells and restore my skin to a youthful glow. Fabulous! It was divine timing. I met my husband-to-be, John Platz, only two months later! *"Every good gift and every perfect gift is from above, and comes down from the Father"* (James 1:17).

Esther's prescribed beauty regimen lasted a full year. Can you imagine what 365 facials must have done for her? Yet, when Esther finally appeared before the king, one look at her natural beauty, refined and perfected by the best spa treatment of the region, was not enough to capture the king's heart! Esther's beauty was far more than skin-deep.

The inner radiance of a spirit refined by testing and endurance shone through to enhance her appearance even more than the yearlong protocol of beauty rituals. Esther's true preparation was in her growing faith in God, who, interestingly enough, is never mentioned in this book of the Bible.

I suspect, too, that the king was dazzled by a sense that he could never fully possess Esther. Her beauty came from knowing who she was and Whose she was. She rested in the fact that no earthly being would ever enter the holy of holies—the deepest part of her heart reserved for the King of kings. She was *His* bride. He was, and always would be, her first love. She was merely a reflection of His glory, His purity and holiness.

Kingdom Woman

The reason for much of the disappointment, rejection, and grief in life is the fact that we are splintered and fragmented people. We are chasing our selfish dreams, striving to be "happy," and often disregarding or disbelieving the clear teachings of Scripture. As we study the models sent by the Lord into our lives or study Scripture, we can feel the jagged, broken pieces of ourselves beginning to come together like a huge jigsaw puzzle. There is integration instead of disintegration; a moving forward spiritually; purpose, instead of perplexity. As we mature, our spirits will show evidence of the Holy Spirit's bearing His fruits of *"love, joy, peace, longsuffering, kindness, goodness, faithfulness, gentleness, self-control"* (Galatians 5:22–23). This, too, is a portrait of Esther, a portrait of grace.

Although you and I probably come from different parts of the country, with different backgrounds, and different family connections, God's grace can produce the same spiritual profile in each of us. While He may use others to model godly living, you can also access it directly. His Word is life, and His Spirit teaches and guides us into all truth. Any virtue that does not proceed from a heart that is right with God is no virtue at all. It is a charade. Deep inward cleansing, not just an external "facial," precedes true holiness.

As Francis Frangipane wrote, "We are seeking a level of holiness that brings the glory of God into our lives. For us to reach our goal we must not only grasp this truth, we must grasp the means to fulfill it. The means to holiness is grace. What God's truth demands, His grace will provide."

The only way you will know the voice of God is to know Him. To become women of grace, to live gracious lives, we must first receive grace—the gift we can never earn—then learn how to extend grace to others as freely as we have received.

Queen Esther's Reflection

Spiritual beauty—God's grace within—produces an irresistible fragrance, rising like incense before His throne and drawing others to you and to Him.

1. Read the Old Testament Book of Esther. You can probably finish it in less than an hour!

2. What preparations did God put into place to lay the foundation for Esther's destiny?

3. Name three examples of great wisdom that Esther used in being prepared.

4. In what ways do you identify with Esther?

5. What traits of Esther's character do you want to apply to your life?

CHAPTER 2

God's Finishing School

Glimpses of Grace

"He guides the humble in what is right and teaches them his way."
—Psalm 25:9 (NIV)

Ah—God's school of graces and refining. God's finishing school is a royal academy. The courses are out of this world! Some of the titles of the subjects that are taught are: Honoring Others; Respect 101; Understanding True Authority; Developing Servant Leadership; Answering the Higher Calling to Serve; Becoming the Right Role Model; Living a Life of Integrity; Humility 101; Applying Manners and Graces; Mentoring 101; and, of course, Unconditional Love 101.

These academics and instructions are basic Christianity 101. Every new believer must go through this training to advance in their spiritual growth. God desires to teach, train, anoint, and activate His people to be spiritually educated is the finest instruction you can acquire. God's finishing school is open to all believers. This discipline will prepare you to go before kings—just as Esther did. Because God is love, the banner over everything from Him is grace, honor, respect, and the things that exemplify these traits.

I love pageantry. When I am viewing a military parade, I see the handsome uniforms and the precision of the soldiers marching each in step with the others. It reminds me of people who have learned to come together as a unit and walk in unity with the same mission. God's school of protocol is much like this army of soldiers.

Because we come into this world needing instruction and correction, one of the first things our parents have to do is try to discipline us through love. This is a pattern of Father God. His love is endless, and His discipline is undergirded with love.

I was born into a family of social graces and manners. This etiquette, these rules and disciplines, were taught to me from both grandmothers and my parents. My father was in the State Senate of South Carolina for 49 years. He was the longest serving state senator in the nation when he died 10 years ago. The senate is based on governmental protocol. I observed it from that perspective as well as at home, where the protocol continued. I learned that my parents placed tremendous emphasis on being respectful of others. They taught us children the basic rules for honoring others and coming under the right authority, to know our place—how to fit in. This has served me well all through my life. Not only do I live this way, I have even coauthored a book about it, called *Social Graces*. Protocol and graces are a part of my life.

I also discovered that knowing the basic rules of etiquette was something that I would need to fit in the world. There are reasons why you thank people with a written thank-you note. There are reasons why you serve others before yourself. These things that seem socially acceptable are also godly traits that are a part of the refining of a person. Esther went through a year's training in this particular art. Her loveliness and grace set her apart from the others.

If I had to choose two bits of advice to give to my children, it would be to *embrace a life of humility* and *let love be your banner*. These are the two things that one needs to be a person of grace.

Oil of Myrrh and Spices and Cosmetics

Esther submitted herself to the six months of deep cleansing with oil of myrrh. This was a necessary part of physical and spiritual preparation in the beauty process, a dual cleansing. Then she went through the six months of herbal spices, fragrances, and cosmetic routines.

> *"Now when the turn of each young lady came to go in to King Ahasuerus, after the end of her twelve months under the regulations for the women—for the days of their beautification were completed as follows: six months with oil of myrrh and six months with spices and the cosmetics for women."*
> —Esther 2:12 (NASB)

These regimens were carefully prepared to make Esther as externally beautiful and pleasing as she possibly could be. All the young maidens were given these treatments before they went to see the king. However, when the time came for the king to choose, Esther stood out from the other young women. She had an indefinable characteristic—one that I like to call *grace*. It showed on the exterior, but it flowed from the interior. God had prepared her for just such a time as this, and Esther exhibited a special grace that pleased the king and led him to choose her to be his queen. The grace that God showered on Esther was a foreshadowing of God's most perfect living example of His grace, Jesus Christ. Because Esther lived before Jesus was born, she did not witness the teaching of Jesus and the example of His life and death. But because she was guided by God the Father, she participated in God's grace that was later shown to us fully. We, however, have the unspeakable blessing of learning directly from the example of Jesus.

The Curriculum

What do we learn sitting at the feet of Jesus? We see perfection. We learn to love. We also discover many spiritual keys to success in life. The curriculum is different from that of the world's set of teachings. Jesus teaches us that to become confident, we must depend on God; to gain influence, we must love others; and to become a true leader, we must serve. This is opposite of the worldview on life's success.

Love is the banner over Jesus's ministry. Everything else follows the emotion that is given to us to make us effective wherever we go. When we are taught of God, we are given spiritual principles that have the power to change lives. We are told to give, and we receive. We are also encouraged to forsake the ways of natural man and live a life of grace and love. In God's school of protocol, we learn to forgive and let the past be just that.

I can recall the days when fear and anxiety ruled my heart. I was 27 years old. Fear had such a grip on me that it controlled my life. Panic attacks were a daily reality. The enemy had walked right in my home and created a sense of hopelessness everywhere he could. Those were the worst days of my life. When I became aware of who was trying to hold me back, I asked the Lord to set me free from this torment. As I continued to study the Word of God, I saw in Scripture that God had not given me a spirit of fear, but a sound mind. I saw my way out for the first time.

Esther was a very courageous woman. I know that she must have experienced some fear. Anyone who is called to serve God will experience some form of fear and torment—spiritual warfare.

Esther is a beautiful example of a woman of grace and protocol. Palace protocol was very rigid. There were rules to come before the king. Rules for what a person could say. Court procedures did not allow anyone to just appear unannounced. Esther knew this. She waited until she knew the timing was right. Although smart, accomplished, and prepared, she looked to Hegai to teach her and coach her as to what to do and say. God's plan was to save the nation of Israel through the beauty of this Jewish woman. What a story! What a woman!

I do not know for what you are being prepared, but I can assure you that there is a plan in place that is designed just for you. Every woman is called to be a woman of grace. This woman of grace is prepared in the Word. She will be mentored. She will be in a Bible study desiring to be saturated in God's Word. She will be taught by God through prayer and revelation. She can be easily recognized by "grace anointing," her manners and graces, because they reflect a life of love—honoring others.

> *"The fruit of the Spirit is love, joy, peace, longsuffering, kindness, goodness, faithfulness, gentleness, self-control."*
> —Galatians 5:22–23

Life begins with a seed! A fruit harvest comes from planting seeds. When seeds are properly planted, they will grow and bear delicious fruit. The qualities in Esther's life were seeds of greatness. She was motivated by love and honor. She was disciplined in the graces and possessed an inward peace. Esther also possessed every fruit of the Spirit. This was the secret of her rare beauty. She was tutored by Mordecai to have much more than beauty; she was a woman of great love and goodness. This is what captured the heart of the king. Most great men want what they do not have.

A Galatians 5 woman of grace is a blessing to all who know her. She stands out in a crowd, far above the ordinary person. What makes her different? There is a special anointing about her—a gentleness and grace—that speaks of contentment and goodness. These traits should be envied by today's women. They should desire this more than anything. This woman will be empowered and motivated by love.

Many times the world cannot see the beauty of a woman of grace. They are hidden away from sight. God makes these women invisible to the natural eye, but obvious to the spiritual eye. Esther was tucked away in her village, unnoticed by the people around her. This was God's protection.

Experiencing People of Grace

I recall as a child going with my mother to visit an African American woman of humble means. Since I was only seven years old at the time, my memory escapes me as to why we were there. This woman knew we were coming and had prepared tea for us. Her home was small but very well-kept. The interior was sparely furnished, but she, herself, possessed a certain grace. Wearing a dark suit with a lace handkerchief in her pocket, she was the picture of the gracious hostess. A starched white tablecloth covered her small table, where a presentation of tea and cookies awaited us. This gift of grace and hospitality made me feel special. It also made me mind my manners! This woman's loveliness has stayed with me as a memory of grace

Financial circumstances do not dictate grace. Grace is the essence of a life of love. This woman possessed a certain level of grace that I recognized as a child and have sought as an adult to attain. Desiring to grow in loveliness is a wonderful trait for all women to emulate. Making people feel at ease, at home, and comfortable is extending the hand of the Lord to others.

In a confused world today, how can we women stand out as people of grace and graciousness? I think that today is no different from Esther's time. The secular lifestyle has always been one of self-promotion, greed, jealousy, envy, and revenge. Esther had to step out as an unusual woman of beauty in a day when women were not revered and esteemed. She allowed God to perfect her beauty on the exterior and also the interior. She was everything that humbled a king—God's secret weapon. She was in disguise.

Today's woman can learn from this lesson of Esther. As we become more and more transformed into the image of our Lord, a beauty radiates from within us. We become intriguing by standards other than those the world uses to seduce. The school of grace empowers us to conquer the enemy of God with weapons of mass destruction—the favor of God!

Are you in a job that you really do not like? Do you see wrongs being done to others on a daily basis? Do you feel completely out of place? You are probably sent in, as Esther was, as a secret weapon for God. Do not bolt and run. Ask God to show you His plan for this season in your life. He will. Stay positioned. Pray and ask God to show you how to take down the enemy in this situation. Remember, when that season is over, God will release you. You will know when this is the case.

Knowing the Right Things to Say

As we place Esther under a microscope, we see her sterling qualities. It's apparent that she had the qualities to be a queen. She was clothed in grace, courage, love, and had an obedient heart. She was tutored as to when to speak; what to wear; and, most of all, what to say—or not say. More than all of these virtues, she had made her life available to the Lord.

Esther needed to know all about correctness and decorum—palace politics. She needed to be schooled in social graces. This course is more about honoring and choosing the correct and proper thing to say than the topic to be discussed. Palace protocol would state that the king would speak and the subject would listen. Short and simple. Answer when spoken to!

How many times have you said something that later you regretted just because you felt pressured to speak? This happens more often than not. The feeling of being put on the spot in a social situation to say something substantial is a trap set by the enemy.

My very wise father taught me that it is better to listen than to speak. Speak when you have something to add to the group. But it is best to acquire the fine art of listening first. I am sure this is what Esther learned at the Palace School of Protocol. Learning to be appropriate and moderate in everything that you do and say is a valuable quest. In Esther's case, it saved her life.

Let's face it, women gossip! Call it whatever you want to, but this is a real problem for the female of the species. She talks, talks, and talks some more! When I was born again, I became convicted of the words that came out of my mouth. I realized that I was accountable for every spoken word. I caught myself saying things that could be misunderstood or at least misinterpreted—just as bad. I had to place a guard over what I said. This was a discipline for me.

Overcomplimenting is a form of flattery. This is also a troublesome area for southern women, because we gush over most things. There is a difference in gushing and being deceitful. Flattery, false flattery, is not godly. It is inappropriate in the life of a believer. If you do this, stop it.

Being a woman who keeps a confidence is a godly trait. When you are known as a discreet woman of faith, God can use you to inspire other women. This is such a compliment to who you are and how far you have come.

Some women have gentle natures and are just easy to be around. Others are loud and boisterous, needing refining. If you have been blessed with a soft pleasant voice, then appreciate it and thank God. Otherwise, pay attention to how loudly you talk and the pitch of your laughter. Some laughter is delightfully entertaining, while other people sound like wild hyenas. Watch the level of your verbal communication. We can learn a lot from Esther about communication. She scored a perfect mark in knowing what to say at what level and how long she should speak.

When to talk and when to be silent? So much is written about the tongue. Be still and know. Women have a propensity to talk. Esther guarded her tongue. This may have been one of her greatest assets. When she spoke, the king gave her everything she wanted. She was bold enough to speak her desires, but they were always for others—not special privileges for herself.

Graceful Timing

Timing is so important. When I speak to women, I tell them that God owns all the time there is. Praying for a husband? Don't call things forth out of time. Trust God, and, when the time is right, He will bring all things, including a husband.

Before Jesus was born, the rabbis prayed for the Messiah to come and redeem mankind. But God knew exactly what was needed and whom He would send. In the fullness of time, Jesus came.

As women, we can learn much about hospitality, graces, and proper etiquette, yet miss out by failing to be on time. Life is about timing—the right timing. Being punctual will always be in vogue and honoring to others. It speaks volumes about you! Do you show respect by being a polite guest or do you make everyone wait for you?

I have a few friends who are habitually late. I do not think that they realize the message this sends. It speaks loud and clear . . . *you are not important enough for me to get ready and make the effort to be on time to see you* . . . . It does not honor the friendship. I don't think they are aware that this is what being late means. They just cannot discipline themselves to get going. As my dear Grandmother Williams often said, "Respect others and be on time! Being late is like arriving somewhere with your slip showing!"

Waiting on God's timing is essential for being in place for spiritual connections and blessings. This is why sin is so debilitating. It keeps us off time, out of step, and away from the generous blessings of the Lord on our lives.

Grace Under Fire

Haven't you always heard that who you are will come out when you are under pressure or under fire? It's amazing what people can say or do when the heat is on. I have heard people lose their tempers in stores and public places over almost nothing. It is embarrassing. Completely inappropriate.

Here's an example. My husband and I like to eat at the OK Café in Atlanta, where they have home cooking at its finest. John and I know all the staff. Customers sign a list and wait to be called to be seated. When a table is available, the greeter calls the customer's name. This particular evening, when our names were called, a woman jumped up and demanded: "We were here first. I saw them come in after us!" She made a huge deal out of it. I immediately responded, "Please, let her go before us." Then the greeter kindly explained that there were two of us and four of them. We were being seated at a table for two. I smiled at the woman who was only slightly embarrassed. She should have been really embarrassed because she had behaved very inappropriately!

I didn't know her then, but over the years I have seen her everywhere—even at her church where I had been invited to speak. I know that she hates that I saw her act like that, but she cannot change that first impression.

We live in a busy world with lots of rude people. But we can make a difference! We can choose to be kind and a person of grace. I have a saying that I have passed on to my two grown daughters and their children—*Manners will take you places that money and education often cannot.*

As women of grace, we need to check this about ourselves. If you have a tendency to be rude, snappy, or have no patience, then you need more refining. This is an area that has not been spiritually developed in you and certainly has not come under the authority of the Lord. Make this a top priority. How you respond and the actions you take tell more about you than anything you can try to say.

Choose your words carefully. Let praise come from your lips—true words of gratitude. Protect yourself from being disorganized and confused. Plan ahead. If you have a tendency to be late, start out ahead of time. Factor in your ability to get distracted as you leave your house. Quit giving excuses. Above all else, do not tell a lie to cover a sin.

Joseph's true character was apparent when he saw his brothers for the first time in line to receive the grain. He wept. His life's calling was greater than his hurt and rejection. Esther was willing to go when Mordecai said go. She had perfect timing because she had studied the king; she was prepared to do her purpose.

We all want to be people of grace. Some fall short because of unbridled anger, fear, and lack of courage. Others allow sin to bog them down over and over again. They seem to never get out of the mire and sin pattern. They are victims of themselves. Some people need a lot of healing. So keep this in mind when you are tempted to have a short fuse with someone else.

When we are put to the test, what do we do? This is a thermometer of how well we are doing. Watch your reactions. Pay attention to how you feel. Do you stress or overreact? The more mature you become in your walk with the Lord, the more refined you will become in everything that you do; your reactions will become milder, your body less tense, and your faith more apparent.

Graduation

As Esther graduated from the protocol school, she knew that the real test was ahead. As each day played out, she would patiently remember all that was taught to her. She knew that every word spoken, every eye contact, and every opportunity to listen instead of talk would be observed by others.

Every day we have a chance to add grace to our lives. Each day has the promise for good or evil. The choices that you make today determine your tomorrows. "Choose you this day whom ye will serve," says the Lord through Joshua 24:15 (KJV).

QUEEN ESTHER'S REFLECTION

Allowing God to refine you will be the beginning of maturity. Being taught the ways of God will put you in the place where others glean from your wisdom. God's School of Graces will prepare you for kingdom living.

Study Guide

1. What are the areas of outright disobedience in your life?

2. What do you need to do to refine and change for His glory?

3. Have you noticed growth and maturity in your spiritual life? How?

4. Make a list of things you would like to change about your social skills.

5. Who are the women of grace that you admire?

CHAPTER 3

Quest for Excellence

Glimpses of Grace

"The Lord does not see as man sees; for man looks at the outward appearance, but the Lord looks at the heart."
—1 Samuel 16:7

AHASUERUS'S KINGDOM-WIDE search for a new queen—127 provinces, remember—combined all the elements of contemporary beauty pageants, reality TV, and high drama. Imagine the excitement when the news came that officers in each of the provinces were being appointed to scout out the most beautiful young women of every village and vale and escort them to the capital city of Susa. The prize that would go to the winner was not a trip to Cancun, but a royal crown and co-regency with the king of Persia! If girls of that day were anything like they are now, I can just hear the hysterical squeals and shrieks. The entire empire must have literally echoed with them. Some lucky girl—the loveliest, the most appealing, the best choice—would soon marry Prince Charming and live happily ever after.

Aren't we all looking for the best? The best spouse? The best address? The best friends? The best bargains? We don't want to settle for second-best or mediocre or even just OK. We want the best—of whatever it is—we can find or afford.

Or what if you or I were the object of the search? Would a king or even a count, desiring to select a bride—providing you were available—ever glance in *your* direction? Would *I* be first pick on the women's steering committee at the church? First chair in the symphony? First callback after the audition?

Would God ever think of you or me when planning a major campaign to save an entire nation from certain genocide? He thought of Esther. So don't be surprised when He calls on you. God calls us to excellence, to be the best at what He's called us to be. He has the best plan for us, and the best life as a result of following Him. You may feel like an unlikely candidate, but God is calling you to be the best, just like Esther.

And just how did an ordinary woman, an orphan with no title or connections, become queen of Persia? How was she able to hide her true identity as a Jewess—an "enemy of the state"? How did she fascinate the king? What did she say or *not* say to become such a powerful vessel for God? Why did He choose her in the first place?

Esther is one of the first people I want to meet when I get to heaven. She has so impacted my life that I want to learn her secrets and thank her for the inspiration she has given all of us. But we don't have to wait until we get there. Esther speaks through her story. Her message to today's contemporary Christian woman can be perceived if we read with the eyes of our spirit.

Mordecai and Esther Go the Extra Mile

At the end of chapter 2 in the Book of Esther, a few small verses tell of an incident that sets the stage for all that follows. Esther's cousin and protector, Mordecai, had been staying near the court, keeping an eye out for Esther's welfare. As he sat at the king's gate one day, he overheard two of the king's eunuchs, disgruntled members of his staff, plotting to harm the king. Mordecai got word of the plot to Esther, and Esther told the king about it, giving credit to her cousin Mordecai. The king followed up with an investigation, and the two plotters were hanged on the gallows. The story of the incident was recorded in the king's daily logbook, the chronicle of happenings at the court.

Mordecai is an example of the devoted servant, one who goes the extra mile. He didn't have to visit the court daily to check on Esther's welfare. He could have said, "Well, she's married to the most powerful man in Persia. I can relax now." He didn't have to stick his neck out to report the plot to the king—no one would have been the wiser if he kept his mouth shut. He may have been risking his own safety by getting involved in palace politics. But he knew the right thing to do, and he did it. He also knew that Esther's safety now depended on the well-being of the king.

Esther also pursued the opportunity to raise Mordecai in the estimation of the king. Even though the story says nothing about the king showing gratitude to Mordecai at the time of the incident, a seed had been planted. Later, at a crucial time, Mordecai's action would hold him in good stead with the king. Mordecai and Esther's excellence in personal conduct would later help save their lives.

The Search

Esther had to discover who she was and where she fit into God's plan, and so do we. The journey to know ourselves and understand why we are here is a lifelong pursuit. We are often more of a mystery to ourselves than to others.

Born into the families that God intended, the search begins at birth. Equipped with our parents' DNA, a personality that is given to us by God, and a life plan that includes gifts and talents to help us fulfill His purpose, we start out as infant beings, fresh and new. In the best-case scenario, we are loved, educated, guided, and prayed for by a godly father and mother who have welcomed us into their world. In the worst of all possible scenarios, we are unwanted and rejected from birth, not valued, abused, considered an intrusion, shamed, and humiliated. In either case, the road to the discovery of God's great plan for our lives is a bumpy one, with many pitfalls along the way.

I can remember when I was about Esther's age and wondering what life held: What would I be? Whom would I marry? Most women are fascinated by these two questions, clueless to any grander plan. I was one of them. I did not see my spiritual potential nor did I understand how to prepare for my life's journey. Rather than pursue and search for God's plan, I sat back and observed for many years, not taking an active role in seeking Him—just getting by, simply going with the flow of where secular life seemed to be taking me. It would take many heartaches and reversals before I came into a correction that signified that my search was narrowing and discovery was at hand.

Finding the Rare and Precious

In my profession—interior design—I have learned how to locate the finest in furnishings, home décor, collectibles, and paintings for my clients. What makes some items so precious and valuable? Most objects are revered because of their craftsmanship, age, preservation, and rarity. Years of experience and study have trained my eye to recognize the rare and priceless. Conversely, by studying the original, the real, I can also spot the fake.

If you have ever purchased a cubic zirconium or one of the other diamond look-alikes, you know how difficult it is to tell a CZ from the real thing. Both are beautiful to look at, with fire and brilliance. But CZs are mass-produced in a laboratory, while real diamonds are formed by the prolonged exposure of carbon-bearing rock (coal) to intense pressure and high temperatures deep within the core of the earth. The comparison is obvious. The random gems that require a great deal of time and extreme conditions to form, plus mining and the fine art of precision cutting after extraction, are far more valuable than those produced in volume in a laboratory. Still, the practiced eye can discern between them.

So it is with people. By fixing our gaze on Jesus—the flawless One—by observing His perfection and purity and studying His integrity and His honest interactions with others while He walked the earth, we can learn to discern the genuine. More than that, we who have received Him as our Lord and Savior are ourselves being transformed from glory to glory into His perfect image!

In searching for the rare, one must realize that the clues to a valuable life are written on the pages of Scripture. We are told everything that we need to think, say, and do in the Word of God.

Often, God challenges us with situations that test our sin nature. When we choose His way, the gates open and we are allowed to come in and discover His true kingdom. When we refuse His counsel, we may spend years outside the gates, looking in—desiring to be seated in the inner courts of the rare and precious.

Are you aware that you have this divine rarity within you? You may not agree, but God says you have it. You were designed to live in a certain generation to accomplish certain things—great things for Him. Take a good look in the mirror. Do you know who you are? What treasure lies within your hands? What has God entrusted to you for His glory? Take a good look! There are precious jewels that God has forged within you like fine diamonds. They must be mined, cut, and polished. The trials and temptations that have come your way, like the intense pressure and heat within the earth necessary to produce a diamond, are necessary for producing a Christlike character within you. Those jewels must be mined by your mentors, cut by the convicting power of the Holy Spirit, and polished to a lustrous sheen by the water of the Word and prayer. Then, at the proper time and in the proper setting, they will come forth, as Esther's did, in a *for-such-a-time-as-this* moment.

Often when mentoring younger women, they ask me how I came to know the Lord. Ironically, my spiritual journey was marked with much pain and heartache. It was only after dragging my heels because of great hurt and rejection that I finally surrendered my very strong, stubborn will to Jesus Christ.

I grew up in a Christian family. I loved everything about going to church, especially "sword drills"—competing with other young people to locate Scripture verses quickly. I knew about Jesus, His family, His ministry, and His death and resurrection. But what it took me years to discover was that, although I knew who He was, I had not *surrendered* my life and will to Him! I knew Him as the historical Jesus, the One in the Sunday School lessons. I believed that He was who He said He was. It would take a tremendous hurt and an emotional fall to bring me to the place where I could see the big picture. I needed a Savior, not an historical figure. This, too, would come.

As a young woman, I loved a good story. Both of my parents were gifted storytellers—beyond the best I have ever heard. Listening to them caused me to have an ear for good stories. My paternal grandmother was a Bible scholar. I remember her discussing the Old Testament with my father, an interest they shared and passed down to me.

The life stories of Joseph and Esther are two of my favorites. Little did I know that these biblical biographies would come back to encourage and inspire me as an adult, to point me to godly examples when I needed more courage, and to provide a credible resource when I mentored others. Really, they would do more than that. God used them to bring healing in my life.

The Bible is the written wisdom of God, sacred and true. A lifelong love for the written Word of God is probably one of the most important character traits one can possess. As you grow spiritually, "mining" the Word, the basic truths take on much deeper meaning.

Thirty years ago, when my life was being put back together after a failed marriage and a season away from God, I was led to read and immerse myself in the Scriptures. I cried out to God for restoration—for His correction and the right pathway. I spent hours upon hours reading and praying for revelation. I returned to church. I joined a Bible study, delving into the Book of Romans for a year. It was manna from heaven for me. Not only was I hearing the truth, but the Word of God was healing my broken, fractured heart. His promises, which are true, began to heal me emotionally. Because I believed what the Scriptures say about faith, hope, restoration, and rebirth, I became a new person. I was redeemed from my sin and set free to live the abundant life.

Becoming a Christian radically changed everything. I went from being an insecure, divorced mother of two small daughters to becoming a believer in miracles. The reason is because I *was* one! Then it was the most natural thing in the world to desire to be more and more refined, healed, and freed to be about His business rather than mine. I want my Lord to feel pleasure in what I do and how I think, and to trust me with those who are as fragile as I was.

You can see why I am so passionate about the Word of God! It is life to all who embrace it. The instructions within those pages are for every need that you have, every question you would ask God, and for every generation, regardless of what is going on in the world. Esther's story is for today!

Raising the Bar

One of the things Esther discovered when she entered the palace program was that the bar had been raised. More would be expected of her. It was a new day, with a different set of rules. This meant that a higher protocol was in effect.

Raising the standard is also part of spiritual growth. The call of the King of kings is higher still, and His expectations are greater. No more observing from the sidelines. It is a new and different day with unique obstacles and more glorious results.

When I realized that I needed to return to the Lord, I began a quest that, to this day, has kept me hungry and thirsty for more of Him. During the early stages of my restoration, my core values were reshaped. My thinking was transformed as I read the Word, heard the truth from Bible studies, and received instruction from my pastor's sermons. Things were changing. I was changing. I was walking in a new freedom. I could feel healing taking place.

Esther's life began to change when she reached the palace. There, beauty regimens were performed on a continuous basis. With a teachable spirit, Esther was ready and willing to be prepared inside and out to please the king. So are we. This is what we experience as we are refined spiritually. We read God's Word and pray. We come into a regimen of placing ourselves in His hands to be fashioned more beautifully and molded into His likeness, much like a rare beauty treatment. The love and light of the Lord become apparent to others around us.

Transformation brings change, of course. Spiritually transforming love can cause you to see truth, and so, desire to rid yourself of all the poisons of the past. We begin to clean house, literally and spiritually. There are some things that just have to go. We talk differently. Gone are the harsh accusations, curses, gossip, and negative confessions. They do not fit into this new level of seeking. When you begin to be aware of this evidence of change, you will know you are growing to look more like Jesus.

A supernatural shift takes place when we receive Jesus Christ as our Lord and Savior. We become eternal residents of heaven, but God also moves us into a new place on earth—for His purpose. We want to be where He desires us to be. A whole new address—a new neighborhood. The old desires for the former places, playmates, and playgrounds are gone. Instead, new people and places become evident. There is a new set of rules—eternal rules. You are in the palace school, being tutored and mentored by God Himself.

Preserving Timeless Traditions

Even after being selected to the palace school of protocol with the possibility of becoming queen, Esther never forgot who she was—a Jewish woman. She also did not forget her people. God placed a love for Israel within her heart. The traditions and prophecies of her spiritual heritage remained in her thoughts and prayers. Her training and mentoring had prepared her to stand in the gap for her people.

How many times have you stood alone in spiritual proxy for your family? If you have not yet done so, get ready! God will use you to be salt and light to those nearest and dearest to you. When the world and sin have wreaked havoc with your marriage, when your children have been in gross rebellion, or when you have been left out of the will, you will call out for help from God. There are so many times when as Christians we are the lone ones to hold onto the horns of the altar. The storm can be so fierce that all we can do is cry out, "Abba, Father!"

Women are called to be keepers of the faith, mothers in the spiritual lineage of the world. We are to preserve the holy and the righteous. We are to do as Esther did and come under the authority of the Lord and under those whom He has placed over us. It is there that we are our most powerful. God uses obedient people to do great things for Him. Esther models this so beautifully. Not only did she preserve tradition, she preserved Israel!

Each of us has a spiritual heritage. We are a part of a much larger plan and legacy of God. Just as Joseph was the great-grandson of Abraham, you will be the mother, grandmother, and great-grandmother to many who are called to do great things for God. The choices you make today will affect your entire family. The healing you receive now will be a channel of healing for the generations to come after you.

Esther's ability to win the heart of the pagan king was her assignment. She was a woman with an important mission—an appointment with destiny.

You, too, have a spiritual destiny with a purpose. Just as Esther was placed in Persia for a time and a purpose, so God has placed you where you are. You may not understand His timing or the season you are in, but God is unveiling and revealing many people of destiny. You and I fit into that plan. He will call us forth and lead us to our place.

When Our Best Is Not Good Enough

The natural man strives to succeed. The very best that we can do and achieve *in our own flesh,* however, is never good enough. It is foolishness to God. So many otherwise "good" people believe that good works buy acceptance into heaven. But our grandest effort is nothing more than a pitiful substitute. Our *"righteousnesses are like filthy rags"* (Isaiah 64:6).

Spiritual excellence is found in relationship with Jesus Christ. He is our Redeemer, Savior, and Elder Brother. His righteousness makes our efforts good enough. Esther understood spiritual excellence. Esther found favor everywhere she went—favor with Mordecai, favor with Hegai, and favor with the king. Through her graciousness, willingness to submit to the beauty regimens, her kindness, and her great beauty, Esther used the gifts God gave her. The resulting favor gave Esther high visibility within the core group of beauties. *"A gracious woman retains honor"* (Proverbs 11:16).

If you have not done so, pray for revelation of your flaws and spiritual weaknesses. When you come to a time when you recognize them, as I did, only then can you invite the Lord to begin His refining process. We women struggle with so many things. We may talk too much. We may be jealous of what others have, even their spiritual gifts. We may resent our pastor, his wife, the elders, ministry leaders, anybody else walking by us at church. We may keep making the same mistakes over and over. We are not prepared to be presented to anyone in the mess we are in. We are not ready for marriage, not ready to be mothers, and not ready to lead others. We need training in palace protocol to prepare for our audience with the King.

God's Perfection

I can remember before I surrendered to the Lord the faulty plans for my life. What was I thinking? I missed the mark so many times. I refused to walk in the spiritual place where God planted me. Instead of embracing my faith, I chose to turn from it and go into Egypt for a season. It was my freshman year in college. I was on my own for the first time in my life. I was wooed by the glamour of cocktail parties and fraternity parties. I wanted to be sophisticated. I temporarily walked away from my destiny.

I was the opposite of Esther. My rebellion caused me years of pain and heartache. If only I had paid attention to her life of discipline and obedience, I could have gleaned so much from her. Instead, I married early and jump-started my life into a future that was doomed for failure.

How many of you fell for that lie? Did you even pray about your future husband? I didn't. It never even occurred to me. I encourage young girls to pray for guidance in that area. Next to your salvation, whom you marry is the second most important choice you will ever make. Your destiny will link up with that person's destiny. A wrong choice will take you far away from the plan of God.

I tell many women who are coming to the reaping phase of the sowing and reaping season in their lives, thank goodness for God's plan B! He knew that we would fall short in every area. So He set in place a Savior—His only Son, Jesus Christ—to redeem us from hell and destruction. But only for those who have eyes to believe and a heart to surrender.

Esther was a "savior" for her people. When the king of Persia issued an edict that all the Jews should be destroyed, only one person stood in the gap for the children of Israel…Esther, a woman of courage.

QUEEN ESTHER'S REFLECTION

Searching for life's answers in the wrong places leads to connections with wrong people, wrong places, and wrong outcomes. Finding rare treasures in life are linked to godly pursuits and eternal treasures. Search for the riches from God with all your heart.

1. Read the Bible every day. Start this day by reading again the Book of Esther. Read slowly, and ask God to give you revelation knowledge about this remarkable woman.

2. Write down the rare and precious traits of Esther that you learned from this chapter.

3. How can you relate to Esther at this place in her story?

4. What areas of excellence is God building in you? How is He doing this?

CHAPTER 4

Esther's Secret Weapons— Prayer and Fasting

Glimpses of Grace
"Then I set my face toward the Lord God to make request by prayer and supplications, with fasting, sackcloth, and ashes."
—Daniel 9:3

THERE WAS nothing ordinary about Esther of Persia—her physical appearance, her conservative use of words, her ability to wait patiently, her quiet courage, her graciousness. This woman of destiny, though no one would have suspected it at the time, was "queenly material" from birth. Hidden beneath her beauty and grace were some secret weapons—weapons of wisdom and deep spiritual significance that initially went undetected by the natural eye.

God has often chosen the foolish things of the world to confound the wise. Deposited in the most unlikely places are treasures for those who can see with spiritual eyes. Esther was such a treasure.

To participate in the royal beauty pageant, the winner of which would be crowned queen of the whole realm, each maiden had to be trained in the politics of the court. Along with the other contestants, Esther was tutored in every aspect of royalty. She was as fully prepared for this new role as possible. Yet please do not underestimate the times. This woman was a minority within a minority. First of all, she was a female in a male-dominated society, where women were easily overlooked, dismissed, even exterminated. Second, she was a believer in the one true God, a Jewess living among pagans. Exposure at any time could mean death. Not only could she lose the crown, she could lose her head!

To survive in this climate and culture, one must exercise great wisdom and restraint. Esther knew this. Among all the women who talked too much and too long, she did not broadcast her business. She operated under the radar, going about her training diligently and discreetly, yet never forgetting her roots.

A New Villain

After Esther became queen, her safety and well-being were ensured, right? Wrong. As queen, Esther faced a double-edged threat to her life that brought her to her knees. She still held secret the fact that she was a Jewess, but as events unfolded she was forced to choose between revealing her secret or watching the destruction of all her people and living out her days in fear of being exposed and killed.

Who brought about these events? The evil Haman. Haman was a member of the court whom King Ahasuerus had made grand vizier, second-in-command, over all Persia. The king ordered all the people in the kingdom to bow and do homage to Haman whenever he passed, and Haman delighted in his importance. He already had extensive lands and riches, and now he had the pleasure of seeing everyone in the empire bow to him wherever he went.

Everyone except one. Mordecai, who was still at court every day, refused to bow to Haman. At first, Haman didn't notice. The king's servants, however, saw it happening again and again, and asked Mordecai why he refused to bow. His simple response was that he was a Jew. The king's servants decided to stir the pot. They brought the situation to Haman's attention. Haman was immediately furious, and the battle lines were drawn. But Haman restrained himself. He waited. He decided he would not only have Mordecai's life—he would wipe out all the Jews in the Persian Empire.

Why was the enmity between Haman and Mordecai so instantaneous and so intense? Some say it was a centuries-old conflict springing back to life. Haman was said to be an Agagite, a member of a group with which the Jews had a bitter blood feud. When Haman the Agagite saw that Mordecai was a Jew, the ancient flame of hatred sprang up between them. Others say it was simply an arrogant, insecure man's anger at a subject's refusal to bow, and his attempt to wipe out any others who might have the same reason to defy him. Whether Haman's hatred was vast and old or new and very personal, it was about to have wide-ranging effects on the Jews in Persia.

Haman went to the king and let him know that "a certain people"—he never named the Jews—were disobeying laws of the kingdom. He asked for permission to destroy them. He also threw some money into the mix—if the king allowed him to do this, he would pay a vast sum of money into the king's treasury. The king blithely gave him permission, threw in his signet ring, and said Haman could even keep his money.

In the king's name, Haman wrote a decree ordering that the Jews of all the provinces—including women and children of any age—were to be killed, destroyed, and annihilated on the day that was chosen. He cast lots, or *pur*, to determine the day they were to be destroyed. (The Jewish celebration of Haman's defeat is called the festival of Purim for this reason.) The reward for the citizens of Persia was permission to plunder all the possessions of the Jews they killed. Does this remind you of any twentieth-century attempts to annihilate the Jews?

When his work was done and all the provinces had been thrown into an uproar by the strange decree, Haman and the king sat down to have a drink. Hmmm. Cheers!

The Challenge of a Lifetime

Esther, residing safely in the palace, was unaware of these events until she heard that her cousin Mordecai was wailing in front of the king's gate, wearing sackcloth and ashes, the traditional way of expressing deep grief and distress. When Esther was told that Mordecai was wailing and crying outside the palace gate, she sent her servant to send some clothes to him. This was embarrassing. She could not imagine what he was doing! In return, Mordecai sent her a copy of Haman's decree. He asked the courier to urge her to go to the king and plead for the lives of the Jewish people.

Esther, our portrait of courage, was still a living, breathing, human woman. She hesitated. She lived every day at the king's pleasure, and she was daily aware of the risk to herself if she displeased the king. The name of Vashti must have served as a constant reminder of the precariousness of her position as queen. And this new decree only served to strengthen her awareness of her husband's capriciousness. Esther wanted to live! So she and Mordecai, through a trusted courier, carried on a conversation about how to deal with this situation.

She laid out her concerns for him. "Look," I imagine she said, "Everyone knows there is a law that if anyone goes into the inner court without being summoned, that person is to be immediately killed. The only way that person gets to live is if the king holds out his golden scepter to them. I risk death by merely walking into the king's presence. I might never even get the chance to speak to plead our cause."

Esther also had another concern. "The king hasn't asked for me for 30 days. I don't know whether he is tired of me, or angry at me, or merely distracted by other things. I don't know whether he will be pleased to see me or whether he will consider me just another queen with too much mind of her own."

Mordecai's reply was the challenge of Esther's lifetime. He began with dread—"Esther, don't think that because you are queen, you are different from the smallest Jew in the provinces who is facing death. You are facing death too. If you remain silent now—" and then he spoke his faith "—deliverance for the Jews will come from somewhere else. But you will have missed your opportunity." Then he put the challenge squarely before her: "Who knows? Maybe you have come to this place just for such a time as this." Mordecai's words, "for such a time as this," ring through the ages as a great biblical testimony to the power of God's purpose in a life. Esther knew she had found hers.

Her decision made, Esther took command. Reversing their usual roles, Esther gave terse instructions to Mordecai. Before she risked her life, she planned to prepare herself spiritually to take this leap of faith. She told him to gather all the Jews in the city for a three-day fast in her behalf. She planned to fast inside the palace, along with her maids, and after three days, she would go to the king.

The Secret of Powerful Prayer

When I first came back to the Lord more than 30 years ago, a beloved mentor advised me that if I expected to grow spiritually beautiful, I should practice two important disciplines: reading the Word of God and spending regular time in prayer. At that time, I didn't know much about either one; although I would have argued that I had read my daily Bible readings from childhood, and I could recite the Lord's Prayer and the Twenty-third Psalm by heart. I would later learn that it is possible to read the Bible all the way through, memorize many passages, and still never do more than skim the surface. Prayer, too, can be entirely superficial—all talk and no waiting to hear what the Father has to say.

There is something about desperation, however, that sends believers to their knees. Esther's life was in jeopardy from the beginning of her association with the king of Persia. From the contest in which she was pitted against the most beautiful young women of the region to the royal wedding and beyond, that first year was a moment-by-moment exercise in patience and courage. She was tutored by her cousin Mordecai, who surely reminded her to practice her Hebrew faith—including prayer.

Along the way, she also submitted her natural desires for food and drink to the practice of fasting. In fasting—abstaining from food for a period of time in order to hear more clearly from the Lord—one focuses time and attention on Him rather than self. Fasting means denying the flesh in order to develop the spirit. Prayer moves us out of the natural realm and into the supernatural, but prayer *with fasting* can produce an even greater connection with God.

For those who are suspicious of fasting and regard it as some kind of religious ritual, I would recommend reading the Scriptures pertaining to fasting. Fasting is not a meaningless external ritual, but an internal spiritual commitment.

As believers, we are told that some of life's breakthroughs come only by prayer and fasting.

Prayer with fasting is the most powerful way of praying. Withhold food and pray. Scripture tells us some things cannot be changed without prayer and fasting. This is an incredible spiritual experience. When I fasted, God began to give me spiritual clarity. One of the things you realize is how controlling food is.

Fasting enables us to see things in the Word. You move into another realm with the Lord. Use this fasting time to really pray. It will take you to the next level of prayer. Prayer and fasting will break strongholds in your life. It moves the heart of God. Esther knew that. Mordecai told her, I am certain.

Today more than ever, we as Christians are clearly being called to fast. This kind of prayer is powerful: for our country, terrorism, revival, and so many important issues and needs.

Kinds of Fasting

1. You could fast one meal a day for a certain period of time.
2. You could fast from morning until dinnertime. (It's key to remember to pray during the time you would have spent eating.)
3. Some have tried a 40-day fast tied into a scheduled Bible reading and prayer. Rick Warren gives an example of this in his book *The Purpose-Driven Life*.
4. Another kind of fast is fasting from media—television, radio, Internet, and other outside influences.

What are the results of fasting? Discipline and control are rewards of consistent fasting. Fasting unleashes the power of God in your life and breaks strongholds. If you want to learn more about prayer and fasting, I suggest you read:

God's Chosen Fast by Arthur Wallis; *The Purpose-Driven Life* by Rick Warren; and *Celebration of Discipline* by Richard Foster.

Learning to Communicate with God

Prayer is spiritual communication. We pray—God listens. Intimacy comes from this relationship of devotion through the act of speaking with God. Communication is a two-way form of connecting. Learning to talk to God and hear from Him is vital in spiritual maturity. How can we achieve this? First you must know Him.

Learning to listen is powerful. I believe that this may have been one of Esther's finest traits. Listening instead of talking prepares one to grasp what needs to be communicated. If you are a talker, become a listener. It is such a compliment to give someone the opportunity to speak to you and really listen to them.

In learning to communicate with God, start a prayer journal to document your prayers. I encourage new believers to do this. As you note your prayers and God's responses, it is plain to see that God does answer your prayers.

The Power of the Quiet Place

Many people avoid being alone. They deliberately crowd their lives in order to escape loneliness or to delay facing some sin or shortcoming. They gravitate to groups where there is so much going on that they have no time for reflection. Through His Word, God calls His beloved ones into fellowship with Him. It is in this stillness that He talks to

His people. It is when we are quiet and in a state of rest that His voice comes through.

Why a quiet place? The Scripture comes back to me: *"He maketh me lie down in green pastures. . . . He restoreth my soul."* Quiet places are places of refreshing to those who want to reflect or hear that still, soft voice. Quiet places are also where we gather our thoughts away from the noisy world. Do not avoid being still or being quiet. Ask God to show you how to quiet your world.

There are so many times when I desire rest. I yearn to be at home with my feet propped up on a favorite footstool. I yearn for this kind of rest in the Lord. This kind of rest is a new level of trust where we release our hopes, dreams, and cares to Him for His safekeeping. I have experienced this quiet place, where God seems to cover me with a soft blanket, and I nestle close to Him and commune with Him.

Strangely enough, there is power in being still. I can think of a verse in Scripture that says, *"Be still and know that I am God!"* Wow! Instead of exhausting yourself with noise and the interference it brings, simply be still—and know! In this state of serenity you will experience a calm, a quiet, a settling. To receive from the Lord, one must learn to be comfortable in this state of stillness.

There is a grace in being still. There is rest in being still. The Lord speaks often in such times of quiet in secret places—places of reflection—gardens of rest and comfort. Seek the wisdom to wait on the Lord in a still place. There is a supernatural power in waiting on His timing. The Lord speaks to me in this mountain place. He says, *"Ann, I love you. You are mine. Come away with Me."*

How to Stay in the Presence of the Lord

The first thing you can do to stay in the presence of the Lord is to stop sinning. Most people do not want to go this far! It's difficult to tune out the world. Turn off everything that distracts you. Start with the television, the radio, the telephone—even the cell phone—and especially the Internet and video games. Begin to control your world by taking over the places where the enemy would pull you off-focus. Start reading and reflecting on the Word of God. This causes you to be realigned. New Christians should spend a lot of time reading the Bible. I prefer reading the Bible to reading self-help books. The greatest lessons are in the Bible.

1. Make time in your schedule—don't wait for elusive "free time."
2. Create a special space for prayer away from the distractions of the world…a corner of your family room, a chair and ottoman, wherever.
3. Turn off the TV and music (even praise music…yes, praise, there is a time for that!).
4. Insulate your world—isolate yourself away from possible interruptions.
5. Don't allow intrusions of the world to come in…sanctify your quiet time.
6. Consider talking to the Lord just before you go to sleep.
7. Mornings can be very special for prayer and Bible reading.

God is always on time for a prayer meeting with you. He will take you and cause you to love the unlovable and bend you so you will become more flexible. Every time I think I've arrived, He opens another door to show me where I can grow. The latest lesson He has given me is the awareness that I need the ability to love more. I need to realign my thoughts and accept His grace to help me to love more deeply, especially those who have hurt me.

Whatever it is, He's doing it, and it's causing me to be a better person. He is requiring me to be more compassionate. This is not easy for me. I have the tendency to hold a grudge—a silent deadly grudge. When I have been wronged, I remember it—for a long, long time. I need more mercy toward those people.

God is requiring more of me at this time in my life. He is not allowing me to hold on to past hurts. I know that I'm getting ready to fly in another direction. I sense the change around me. I feel that I am on the threshold of another world—out of obscurity. We all can be Esthers, people used of God in a clandestine way. We don't even realize it until it's *palace time.* Isn't it amazing and wonderful how we fit into God's overall plans and purposes?

Preparing the Set-Apart Place

Every home should have a sanctuary reserved for time alone with the Lord. This can be a chair in a living room, or the breakfast table, or a corner in a not-often-used guest room. Wherever you decide to meet with Him, make it a quiet place where you can pray and worship.

What keeps our sanctuary holy? Love, commitment, prayer. Prayer is a covering that can come over your life like a mantle. Almost palpable, you can touch it. You can walk under it. Those who come under your prayers can take it away with them.

In the Old Testament, the men of God would pitch a tent and then make an altar to God. I have always loved the romance of the Scriptures, especially about the devoted giants in the faith. Moses led the people of Israel and they wandered around for 40 years. I can visualize this spiritual giant setting up his sanctuary at each stop. He knew to worship God!

In my home, I have several places of sanctuary. My place of prayer is in my bedroom. My place of ministry is in my family room. My place of Bible study is in my office. My sanctuaries are taking over my house!

Take inventory. Look around your home. Where are the places that are perfect for intimacy with your Lord? Prayer places—these places becomes blessed. They become blessed when visited by others and prayer wells up inside them. When people visit you, they feel that God meets with people here.

Esther was a praying queen. Her prayer life changed the history of the world. Esther could have ignored the danger of her people. She could have said that she was not related to them. She could have been eccentric, refusing Mordecai's instructions. She could have pulled the palace curtains and said, "I don't want to be interrupted."

Power Tools for Prayer

Understanding the different kinds of prayer is key to your spiritual growth—prayer can be spoken words, writings, words put to music, Scriptures, and deep intercession where no words are necessary. Do not limit the way you speak with God!

Precious to me are the words that became the prayers my two daughters spoke when they first began to pray. Innocent in the way they talked with Him, I would smile as I heard them dialogue with the Ancient of Days. I thought that He must be greatly amused. Things like, "Hi, what are you doing up there?" or "Are you all by yourself tonight?"

If you are committed to a deep relationship with the Lord, spend a lot of time in prayer. As you start understanding the value of prayer, it will increase your devotion to God. When you move into true ministry, you realize that you have partnered with God, trusting Him to that level.

Closing Out the World

Understanding the importance of closing out the noise of the world is another key to true intimacy in prayer. Covenant relationship requires this. Redeemed, we're in the beloved. In this place of divine protection we see, hear, and know Him as Father and provider. Unless we are willing to come away with Him, we will never know Him in His fullness!

When we are being wooed by the Spirit of God, it reminds me of being courted. When you fall in love, you want to be where that person is. You want to close out the world and share your life. Time stands still. Your heart beats only for that person. The act of falling in love with the Trinity is the ultimate love—a true divine romance.

Love? Yes, the greatest love there is! God has called me to come into a special place with Him. He will not let me have my way. In that place of prayer, He loves me so much that He will not allow me to miss my calling. Something will happen and my "natural man" will react. Then I think—why is this coming back? I have dealt with that. I am disgusted that I have taken some steps backward! Then the Lord pulls me back into that intimate place with Him—that Father-daughter place of peace. There He comforts me as no other love can. Get into the loving protection of the Lord and healing will take place.

There are times when we need to sit alone in that sanctuary—count our blessings, recall what God has done. I remind women in crisis that they need to look back at what God has done for them in the past. The Lord has a great track record of being faithful to all of us.

Mentored in Prayer

Prayer—what a huge subject! What a huge spiritual connection, a kingdom connection. Prayer is the most powerful communication there is. I love to pray. As I have learned how to pray, I spend much time in prayer. The older I get, the more I pray. I love this time with God. I also know by now, thank goodness, that I need to ask God for help—His divine assistance.

I believe that if we could see the effect that prayer has, we would pray as much as possible. Using Jesus as an example of a person who prayed, we should pray as He prayed—often and with a sincere knowledge that God is for us!

One of the first spiritual teachings I received from my mentor, Eliza, was an instruction to pray about everything. When I would ask her a question, she would say, "Darling, pray and ask God! And come back and tell me what He says!"

At first I thought this was unusual, but as I got to know Eliza, I realized that she was dead serious. She wanted me to have intimacy with God! This is what a mentor should do. Teach younger women how to pray. This has been an invaluable lesson for me. It structured my prayer life. I know to instantly pray.

Eliza was mentored by a wonderful woman, Mildred Singleton, from Troy, Alabama, who lived in Nashville. When they first started their mentoring relationship, Eliza told me, she would ask where something was found in Scripture. Mildred would tell Eliza where it was. Finally, knowing that Eliza was becoming too dependent on her, Mildred said, "Look it up yourself, after all, you have a perfectly good Bible!"

Eliza loved to watch Mildred pray. Mildred would raise her head toward heaven and pray. She never prayed looking down. I asked Eliza what she learned most from Mildred about prayer. The answer was that God always says, "Yes, no, or wait"! Eliza's advice is: "Don't try to push it. What He says is it!"

A Life of Significance

When Mordecai had his discussion with Esther through the courier, he helped her discover the significance of her life. He helped her interpret the events of her life and times in light of God's purposes. Esther saw the danger, and Mordecai helped her see it as God's opportunity for her. After all, he said, isn't it possible that all the unusual events of your life have led you right to this moment—because God put you here for this purpose? Mordecai's mentoring made all the difference in her life.

In Psalm 139, Scripture tells us that we are purposed and meant to be here, that our days are numbered, and that every day of our life is recorded. I love this chapter. I love the message God has given here—that no matter where we go, He is there. Every life is significant. Every birth is planned. Every life has a God-purpose.

We all have worldly goals for success, and this can be good—for example, you can become a doctor and aid in healing the sick. Whatever profession you have a talent for, use it. Success is good, but it does not hold any weight in heaven. It is all earthly stuff.

Significance is a higher call of living. It is sacrificial living and giving. This way of life is about all you do for kingdom purposes. These are the things that count. . .these go to heaven with you. Helping someone receive salvation…praying with a hurting friend…mentoring a younger woman in the Lord…presenting the gospel to others…being available to the Lord and making your life count for Jesus.

Look for riches within yourself. Search for the rare and precious. Have the desire to be remolded and refined by the fire of God. Ask God to bring significance into your life. Give Him permission to "weed out the dead parts of your life." He knows what needs to be eliminated.

Ask God to give you royal favor. Ask Him to use your abilities to make a difference in this world. Make yourself available for His use. Allow Him to refine you. Allow yourself to be critiqued. If you truly desire the Esther anointing, then you must begin to prepare to meet the King. You must move into a life of significance.

QUEEN ESTHER'S REFLECTION

Place your trust in the living God through communication—through prayer, fasting, and reading His Word. Give God permission to expand your faith. Trust Him with all that is dear to you. He will open His kingdom to you with favor and grace.

Study Guide

1. How much time do you spend in prayer? Are you satisfied with your prayer life?

2. What do you need to do to give your prayertime more depth?

3. List the quiet places you have established to be with Him.

4. How do you recognize the fragrance of a godly woman? Name some women who fill this bill.

5. What advice do you hear Queen Esther speaking to you through these pages about being a secret weapon for the Lord?

6. Name your personality traits. Write down the godly aspects of these personality traits.

CHAPTER 5

Courage Before the King

Glimpses of Grace

"For we are to God the fragrance of Christ among those who are being saved and among those who are perishing."

—2 Corinthians 2:15

ESTHER FOUND herself in a situation most women will not experience. She had won the heart of a pagan king. She became not only his bride, but also his queen. She was wife of the most powerful man on earth. She was the ultimate royalty—queen of Persia. As the queen of this principality, she was able to influence her husband, the king.

There is more to marriage than meeting your prince charming and planning a wedding. As women, we know this. So many brides get caught up in the wedding ceremony, the romantic feeling that accompanies a wedding, and not realizing that a marriage is going to follow the festivities. If we are not prepared for the marriage, the union will be difficult and, sad to say, may fail—even royal marriages sometimes fail.

Put yourself in Esther's place. She would be the Princess Grace or Princess Diana of her day. Every eye would be on her for the rest of her life. Women would take cues from her. They would pay attention to her clothing, her hair, what she wore, what she spoke, how she honored her husband, and everything she did. All eyes would certainly be on her wedding day and ceremony.

Because she was willing to be taught by Hegai, Esther knew her husband—his favorite foods, his favorite colors, what he thought about women, and certainly what his last wife did that displeased him! She certainly could take cues from the former queen who was "put away" for her disobedience to the king.

Esther had won the beauty contest. Now it was time for the marriage, where the real test would take place. She would face daily challenges as the wife of the king. After all, the enemies of the king were lurking around the palace also. Soon, Esther would have to make the biggest decision of her life. Her subjects were watching her every move.

Timing of the Lord

"God's timing is perfect" is a common saying among Christians, and it is true. So often, events of our lives lead up to a time when God releases favor and blessing. We do not know the mind of God. His timing correlates with His plans. Being in the will of God brings us perfect timing.

Part of Esther's palace training was to observe, learn how to watch patterns, and become aware. One thing that we can learn from Esther is her ability to wait upon God to bring about the perfect timing for her to go before the king. In her case, it meant life or death.

Esther spent three days fasting, and then she went to make her request of the king. What do you imagine were her thoughts during those three days of waiting? She might have imagined what would happen if the king did not hold out his scepter. She might have planned for what she would do if he did hold out his scepter. Once she had his attention, she would have the fearsome task of informing the king that she was a Jewess and finding the most effective way to plead for the lives of her people. And through it all, she had to behave like a queen. Esther's thoughts must have been racing.

Before she went in to the king, Scripture tells us she put on her royal robes. If I were Esther, I might have given a few extra brush stroke to my hair and dabbed on his favorite perfume; wouldn't you? Esther wanted to be as pleasing as possible when she went in to the king. After all, her beauty had gotten her in this position. She needed every ounce of the allure that had won the king's heart when he married her.

And what could Esther expect from the king? We know that King Ahasuerus had a gregarious personality and loved being with people. He certainly had no problem hosting a palace party that lasted for six months! He wanted his friends to be with him. He could be capricious and careless, but he could also be very generous. Along with a great appetite for food and wine, he had the ability to give. This may have been his love language. Whether he was providing a place or giving gifts, he was an unusual king.

Scripture doesn't tell us how Esther felt about her husband, the king. She may have fallen in love with him at first sight. She may have resented the selfishness and weakness he displayed at times. She may have been living her childhood dream or enduring a never-ending nightmare while living at the palace. I hope that God showed Esther the best side of the king. I hope she knew a side of the king that nobody else knew. I hope that God let her have a view from on high of her husband. Love always looks for the best, you know.

Raising the Scepter

After the third day of fasting, Esther rolled the dice. When she went into the inner court and entered the king's presence, Scripture says that she *"found favor in his sight"* (Esther 5:2). He was so pleased to see her that he promised to give her anything she wanted, even up to half his kingdom! Esther couldn't have asked for a better reception. She must have felt relief, but she controlled herself. She didn't fall at his feet, tell him the whole story, and beg for her people's lives. She was a queen, but she was not a drama queen! Instead, she invited him to a dinner party that night—and she invited Haman, as well.

The dinner party was a "banquet of wine," according to Scripture, so the king and Haman must have been pleased by the menu. After dinner, the king again asked Esther what she wanted, again promising up to half his kingdom. Esther replied that, if she had found favor in his sight, her only request was that he attend another dinner party the next night, along with Haman. After that dinner, she would tell him what she wanted. The king agreed.

Haman went home that evening, elated at the special treatment he was receiving from the queen. He bragged to his wife that he was the only person other than the king who had been invited. His vanity was stroked; he was practically purring about it. He had no idea that a trap was being laid for him.

The next night, after another delightful dinner, the king again asked for Esther's request. With great decorum, Esther said to him: *"If I have found favor in your sight, O king, and if it pleases the king, let my life be given me at my petition, and my people at my request. For we have been sold, my people and I, to be destroyed, to be killed, and to be annihilated."* She employed the very three words used to such redundant effect in Haman's evil decree. The king, astonished, asked who would dare do such a thing, and Esther delivered the deathblow to her adversary by simply naming him—*"The adversary and enemy is this wicked Haman!"*

Ladies, that is what I call a dinner party! The king, outraged, ordered Haman hanged, and he was hanged on the gallows he had built for Mordecai. Haman's estates were given to Esther, and she promptly put Mordecai in charge of them. The king was unable to revoke his initial decree, but he gave Mordecai his signet ring and had him write a second decree to be sent to all the provinces, giving the Jews the right to return violence for violence upon any who attacked them on the appointed day of the massacre.

The story ended with all the flourishes of a Hollywood ending! The bad guy was brought down, the good guy was raised up, the husband became a hero in the eyes of his wife, and the innocent victims-to-be were rescued. No one could ask for more. In future years, a festival was instituted commemorating Esther's bold act and the deliverance of the Jews from the plot of Haman—it is known to this day as the festival of Purim.

Courage

In 400 B.C., women were not valued. Most marriages at that time were arranged marriages. Esther's marriage was also arranged, but arranged by God. We don't know exactly what happened when Esther went in to meet the king. She was purposed of God to go in there. The outcome was that she was the agent who stood in the gap, a thin thread that held the Jewish people's lives. God was guiding her.

It takes courage to be different; courage to risk, courage to take a stand, courage to go against the flow. Courage is like a muscle that has to be used to build its strength. The more you use it, the more powerful it becomes. Clearly Esther had the courage to risk and to do it wisely, not foolishly.

Esther's extraordinary life is important in the history of Israel. She is revered as a mother in Israel, one who stood in the gap at a crucial time in the life of Israel. She was an appointed, anointed vessel put in place for a certain time in history. Her every move was strategic for the life of this small nation, the apple of God's eye.

This same kind of anointing or grace-covering is available to all of us. This special blessing—the Esther anointing—is given when we have answered the call to serve God with our lives. When we lay down our plans and pick up God's mapping for our lives, then and only then do we step into that narrow gate of purpose for His glory.

QUEEN ESTHER'S REFLECTION

Allow the Lord to teach you about courage. Open your heart to receive revelation to areas in your life where you need to show courage now. Remember, God goes before you and behind you, as He did for Esther, and you will not be abandoned!

Study Guide

1. Ask God to reveal true courage to you.

2. Make a list of five ways Esther showed courage. In what ways are you like her?

3. There are many different kinds of courage. What kind of courage has God given you?

4. What are you expecting God to teach you through Esther's story?

5. Esther was afraid, but when she knew she had to take a huge risk, she prepared herself carefully. How do you prepare yourself when a situation requires courage?

6. What traits of Esther's do you want to develop in your life?

Part Two

Spiritually Beautiful

"There are two ways of spreading light:
To be the candle or the mirror that reflects it."
—Edith Wharton

CHAPTER 6

Your Home . . . Your Palace

Glimpses of Grace

"Friend, you have no idea how good your love makes me feel, doubly so when I see your hospitality to fellow believers."

—Philemon 1:7 *(The Message)*

A FEW MONTHS ago, a friend came to visit us from out of state. We talked privately for a while, then at the end of our time together, my friend called for his driver to come pick him up. When the driver walked into my home, he looked startled and gasped. Then he blurted out, "There is so much love in this home!"

I was surprised that this young man in his mid-30s would say or even notice this. It was the ultimate compliment. I knew God was showing him something important.

Interestingly enough, he was standing in the room where we meet for prayer. I expected him to compliment the interiors, but he saw deeper than that. He saw what the king saw in Esther, a deeper revelation. He saw the Spirit. He saw the love of God! Oh, to have eyes to see the Lord's gift of love.

For four years my husband; my younger daughter, Margo; her husband, Nelson; and I have had prayer in this room for special people the Lord sends to us. This started in 2002. I had been praying, seeing God's guidance about our family's personal ministry. Each year from Christmas through New Year's, I ask the Lord to reveal to me what He wants our family to do especially for Him in the coming year. It is my Christmas gift back to Him. Many years it has been some form of ministry in our home or some outreach. This particular year I felt that I was to make available two hours a week for the Lord to use our home and our gifts of prayer and intercession to bless His people. Those prayertimes are held in the room that this young man was standing in.

I asked the driver if he would like for me to pray for him. He smiled and heartily agreed. I asked my husband to join me. We began to call forth the blessing of the Lord over his life. We prayed for him to be awakened to the love of God. We asked the Lord to comfort him, help him, bless him, and cause all things to come together for him for God's glory. I also sneaked in a prayer that I wanted the Lord to go ahead and send him a wife. He smiled. I knew that he appreciated me praying for this. After all, a man who has a good wife has a good thing!

At times like this I am so thankful for a home that can be used this way. It is private and set aside for as much prayer and ministry as is needed. I am also glad that I can practice what I preach. I have my home ready in season—at the least amount of notice, I can invite people in for ministry. Early on, I discovered that if I go to sleep with my house in order, I will awaken to a clean home. This is a discipline that I started when I was a single parent. I was ready for the next day. It just made life easier!

Many times I think we underestimate the role of hospitality in the story of Esther. After all, two dinner parties were the dramatic centerpieces of the story. Esther knew how to make her husband feel special and welcomed—and she even knew how to charm her enemy, Haman, so much so that he was bragging to his friends that he was invited to her parties! Yes, Esther definitely had a gift for hospitality, and she used it for God's purposes.

Creating a Royal Refuge for the Family

In planning a home, we think of the obvious things that make a house a home: furniture, curtains, mirrors, lamps, lighting, and so on. Often, we do not make a list of the spiritual things that are needed to accompany these beautiful things. I am especially aware of this as an interior designer. Homes do have feelings and personalities. The young driver was right. Some houses are battle-scarred repositories of hurt, while others almost reach out and hug you.

I offer advice often. As a design professional, I say *make your home your palace*. Keep it clean! Make it beautiful! Make it special. Allow your home to grow with you. Let your faith be evident in every room.

One of my favorite things to do is burn lovely scented candles. I adore them. You should see my friend Cynthia Huffmyer's candles! She has every room in candlelight! Her home is an exquisite country French haven!

I enjoy fragrances, especially floral ones. I appreciate it when friends give me candles. The aroma gives the house another dimension of loveliness, a fragrance. I think that Esther knew this. After all, she was treated to all those beauty routines in preparation for her court date with the king! I am certain that home fragrances were top palace priority!

Women, we can make our homes into places of beauty. It's more than decorating—it's palace making. After all, it is your place. I am only beginning to understand the word *place*. Our surname, Platz, is of German extraction and means *place* in German. *Place* in the natural world means plot of land, particular spot, location, area, or site. In the spiritual world, *place* means dominion, house, residence, and home. Your place is also your purpose and position in life. God has *placed* us so that we may find our *place* for His glory!

Palace beauty is bringing forth excellence, beauty, grace, and comfort. Esther knew this. She was the queen who made a home for her king. There are many unspoken lessons in this analogy. Be a wise woman. Take a good look at your home, what it feels like, looks like, sounds like, smells like—is it "fit for a king?"

How to Honor Those You Love Most

When you love someone, you want to do for them; provide for, serve, and love them. It is just a natural spilling over from your heart to theirs. When I married John, I wanted to create a home of love for him. I wanted our lives to center around our love, mutual faith, and family. John told me soon after we were married that there were two things he did not want: a dog and a boat . . . also no birthday parties. He claimed to be allergic to dogs. And I could understand the boat issue, too much trouble. And the birthday parties could be because he was many years older than me, so I could understand that. Was I WRONG!

When you love someone and they love you, it is hard for them to deny you your heart's desire. I wanted a dog. So, in order to honor his request, I remained silent for 25 years. Those who know me would find it hard to imagine me silent about anything. Finally, last year on my birthday, John asked me what I wanted as a gift. John is practical. He asks, therefore, he knows that I will like whatever he chooses.

Boldly I said, "I really want a dog!" I could hardly believe I had actually said it.

"A what?" John said back.

"A dog! You heard me!" I laughed.

He didn't laugh. "Ann, you do not want a dog. You are gone so much. Who will take care of it?" he asked.

I smiled.

"I do not want a dog," John repeated himself.

I continued to smile. God had placed a desire for me to have a dog. John knew this and had told me earlier that I could have one after he passed away. He was sure that I would get one then.

"What kind of dog?" he asked.

"A King Charles Spaniel!" I smiled.

"I'm not sure that I know that breed. What does it look like?"

I walked over and took down a painting from our family room wall. It was a portrait of this breed of dog, a small dog that looks like a miniature cocker spaniel but has chestnut and pearl coloring.

"When did you get that painting?" John asked.

"We've had it for more than 20 years," I told him. John stared at the painting. He made no comment. The next day when he returned home from the post office, he told me that he had seen a dog like the one I wanted. He even smiled when he told me how cute the dog was. This was a miracle! Then he said, "How are you coming along finding the dog?"

I could hardly believe what I was hearing. I knew that I had to move fast. John was softening. Within hours I had located Lilly. She was at a special breeder's kennel in Missouri. Within a week, Lilly Penelope Platz was in our arms. You guessed it! Lilly bonded to John. She loves me, but she is *his* dog. Lilly loves everything about John Platz! He feeds her, walks her, gives her treats, and she even takes an afternoon nap with him! I knew who was going to take care of the dog while I'm out of town!

Lilly has brought an extra element of love and devotion into a home that was already filled with love. She is even a beautiful accessory, sitting posed on a pillow. We needed Lilly. John needed Lilly. She has filled a place in our lives that we did not even know was vacant.

Lilly has made me aware of all the things that we need. John and I could have lived perfectly wonderful lives without her, but with her we have added so much love! In loving and honoring others in your home, open your doors wide to all that God has for you—even a new pet. Lilly has made me love my home more. Odd as that sounds, I look for ways to make her comfortable! I have provided numerous beds and places where she knows that she belongs. I want to be where she is. Right this moment, she is asleep at my feet—on a velvet dog blanket!

Providing comfort for those you love is mandatory. It is a part of being a gracious woman. Take a look around your house. What do you see? Does your home speak of love? Are your chairs comfortable? Can one take a snooze in your family room? Do you provide comfort for your husband, your friends? Do you have tables next to your chairs for guests to set a drink on?

Preparing the Home

Esther thought like a palace woman. She would tell today's woman to take control over her home. I believe that "home" was her concentration. Accept your power. Do not give it away to others.

For several years I have enjoyed speaking to a wonderful group of pastor's wives. Each year Johnny and Janet Hunt, from Woodstock First Baptist Church in the greater Atlanta area, host a Timothy+Barnabas Ministry time for pastors and their wives. It is a retreat time to allow pastors to be away from their churches. I am one of the regular speakers at this event. I love pastors' wives!

Each year I think of a topic that will allow me to have fun with them, but also give them advice that will help them in their homes and marriages. This year I spoke to them about making a beautiful home. I spoke as a wife, interior designer, and as a mentor/encourager. I share this with you also.

God has given you the most incredible love, nurture, and blessing to be a confidante to a man of God. I can't think of a higher position for a woman. You can build him up or you can do the opposite.

You tear down your husband by criticizing, correcting, making fun of him, telling something on him, embarrassing him. Find a way to praise your husband. Thank him; start making him comfortable the moment he comes home. Help him by having things in order and keeping a clean house. Your husband is coming home after facing a day full of all kinds of problems. Let him come home to a place of peace, where he can be a man.

House Beautiful 101

People often ask me for advice on making a beautiful home. I share with them both the larger principles and the small details, and I see this as a ministry! Imagine how much more peaceful the world would be if our homes were havens of love and faith. Here are some of my favorite tips.

The Master Bedroom. The most important room in the home of a married person is the master bedroom! Period! This room is a place for rest, refreshment, privacy, love, and intimacy (you know there is a difference here). If I were going to have a home project, the master bedroom would be the top priority.

Wise women make their master bedrooms a place of love and comfort. Pay attention to your husband, to what his needs are. Don't drape clothes over a chair or leave a trail of clothing for an imaginary person to pick up after you. No! I was reared this way—not having to clean up, but having someone who came behind me and did this for me. When I married, it was terrible! I had to break those bad habits. I decided early on that I was not going to do that with my children. Bad habits are hard to break.

If you want to love and honor your husband, have a beautiful bedroom that you both can enjoy. Don't you dare buy any 100-watt bulbs for your lamps. No one looks good in harsh light. Lowest wattage, please. This is not an operating room and not a reading room. If he insists on reading in this room, place a floor lamp next to his chair with a three-way bulb or a dimmer.

Eight Suggestions to Make Your House Lovely and Comfortable

1. **Clean your house.** It's amazing what a major cleanup can do. Dust, clean the windows, change the sheets, add soft blankets, and overall pick up the clutter. It can do wonders!
2. **Pick up all stacks.** Remove all stacks of things from bedside tables and major pieces of furniture. This is a command. Find a place for everything or get rid of it. Stacks

of books need to go to a bookcase or shelf. Get them off of the floor and definitely away from the bedside tables.

3. **Remove all clutter.** Junky areas are dust catchers! Try to place as little as you can in your master bedrooms, especially next to your beds. Clean up and clear out!

4. **Get everything in order!** Rearrange your drawers. Also organize your bathrooms and shoe closets. Buy baskets or attractive storage boxes, and use these kinds of storage provisions to organize small items.

5. **Fill in with some nice extras.** Look for trouble spots. Where do you need a small table, another lamp, or a pillow or two?

6. **Arrange your bedroom furniture in the best way.** Place the bed in the right place. Note: The bed is usually placed best if you walk into the foot of the bed as you enter the room. This allows more room in the space as you enter. Watch out for diagonally placed beds. They take up the most room!

7. **Allow your husband to relax in the master bedroom.** If you want his attention, remove all distractions. Try, at all cost, to keep your bedroom from becoming his second office. Do not have a computer in your bedroom!

8. **Make sure your bed is comfortable.**

   a. **Get a comfortable mattress!** There are two major comforts in a bedroom, the mattress and the sheets. These are where I recommend that you spend your money. Be practical—mattress pads and high-quality thread-count sheets. (I suggest above 300-thread count.)

b. **Layer on the love.** A client taught me how to "make a bed!" Start with the bottom fitted sheet, then the top sheet placed on the bed with the wrong side up. Then add a lightweight blanket. On top of that add another top sheet, but this time put it on right side up. To finish off this bed of comfort, put on a *matelassé* coverlet. This is an unlined quilted bed coverlet. All the stores and catalogs have them. They are machine washable! Then, place your bedspread on the top of all of this comfort! Bedspreads are not meant to be a covering for sleep.

c. **Pillows are the perfect accessory for the bed.** There are two kinds of pillows needed for your boudoir—the ones you sleep on and others for extra comfort. I suggest two pillows for each sleeper. One can be down-filled and the other polyester. One gives comfort, while the other gives stability. Then there are the "other" pillows, the smaller back pillows, the neck rolls, and the baby pillows. I love them all! Sometimes it just feels good to place a small pillow under your legs at the knee. When I do this for John, he smiles!

How to Say I Love You *All Over Your House!*

There are many ways to say *I love you* in your home. From three-way lightbulbs to dimmer switches, you can control the atmosphere by controlling how much light and glare enter a room. And there is too much sun and too much glare coming in from the popular, very large, expansive windows of today's homes.

I enjoy finding small treasures that say *I love you*. I adore small sachets that can be placed between pillows or near the bed, preferably in the bed. Lavender scents as well as fragrant flowers make for a lovely scented bed.

One of my favorite bed secrets is Lady Primrose dusting silk. Caroline Hunt from Dallas, Texas, founded *Lady Primrose* with Vivian Young. These two exquisite women have the best line of fragrances for the boudoir. Every reader should rush out and purchase a few of their items for the bedroom. Queen Esther would have had these products delivered to the palace!

These touches of fragrance, sprays for sheets, pink light-bulbs, and other considerations—a CD player for soft music, clock radio, and so forth—all make for a slower pace and conditions for true love and rest to take place. Just remember that the single most important thing that you can have in your master bedroom is love. Place a high importance on your husband. Do not take late-hour phone calls. Leave chatting with friends to daytime hours. Give your man your full attention. Close out the world around you.

The Home as Church

I believe that more and more we will use our homes as a place of church and worship. After all, this is how the first church started. Your home provides privacy. This sets the stage for intimate relationships.

I often hear women tell about the joy of attending a prayer group or Bible study in someone else's home. Why use your home for this reason? I believe that the home of

Christians has a certain anointing that makes it a place for hospitality and love. When you are blessed to have a home that can accommodate groups, by all means open it up for kingdom purposes.

Young people are looking for places to gather. Your home as a place of fellowship is perfect for this purpose. I know that my girls have always enjoyed bringing friends to meet us and have us pray for them. This has been a longstanding tradition in our family.

Esther understood the home as church. She was a great hostess, as we know from the writings in the Book of Esther. Her dinner parties were legendary! She used her palace as a place for God's ministry, even when it meant dealing with the Lord's enemies. Knowing how to use your home is a key to hospitality evangelism. Commit your home and the ministry of your home to God. Then just stand back and see what He does.

I use my home to celebrate friends' birthdays and special occasions. Not only do I celebrate them, I pray for them. I use this time for ministry. After all, it is my house! This would be difficult in a public place or restaurant.

I hope that new opportunities to use your home will come forth for you. Traditional church and home will take on another role. Be open to the moving of the Spirit. Ask God to show you how to prepare your residence and heart for this ministry. He will do it. I believe that churches are going to come into the homes again, as in the early days of the Christian church. Those of us with large homes are perfectly geared for that. What a wonderful opportunity to use what we have! You may look at your home and say, "Why would two people need that much space?" But God can give you the vision for using your home as a pulpit, a place of prayer and instruction, a sanctuary, and a home ministry for people whose lives are at stake. What could be more wonderful?

Preparing Your Home

God calls for women to prepare their homes. Just as we prepare ourselves spiritually, we must do the same thing for our houses. Caring for the home is a privilege. I love doing this. It has been a joy for me to find the treasures for our nest.

Some women are natural keepers of the home. They instinctively know how to apply interior spirit-lifters. These women take control of every area: the noise, the fragrance, the color, the basic needs to get a house in order. But many women feel stuck in getting their homes ready or finished. Whatever you are putting off, do it. Make a list. Get ready. Who knows? You may soon find yourselves entertaining angels unaware.

At the end of each year I make a to-do list of things that I need to do for my home. This list often includes items like paint a room, repair a floor, or some other major need that I must attend to. This is necessary upkeep, and if left undone, may cause you to wake up and realize that you have not properly maintained your home.

Commit yourself and everything else to the Lord—all the chambers of your heart and all the rooms of your home. Then and only then will you feel the presence of God throughout your home. Others will feel His presence there also!

Making God Feel "At Home"

Have you ever thought about what makes God happy about your home? Could it be the sweet spirit that prevails, the music, or the quiet time that you have with Him? So many homes are messy, loud, and not conducive to being ready at a moment's notice to have fellowship.

Do you have sanctuaries in your home? You need places where you can turn away from the stress of the day and be refreshed, either praying or reading the Word. Take a good look around. Start creating those places—honored places where you can entertain the Lord.

Think about what your home says about you and your faith. Go through your books and throw out the ones that are filled with Greek mythology or some non-Christian religion. Get rid of anything with a zodiac symbol or information. Ask God to walk you through the halls of your home and gather up the things that dishonor your Lord. Do the same with your children's books and treasures. Teach them early to have possessions that honor God.

Honoring Others in Our Homes

Grace Kinser was a friend of mine who used her lovely home for ministry. She was well known for her company called Mrs. Kinser's Foods. She was also well known for her faith and love for God. Grace met Kay Arthur when Kay was a young Bible teacher in Tennessee. Kay and her husband, Jack, had just returned from the missions field. Grace, a true Mordecai, saw Kay's teaching potential. With a keen mentor's eye, Grace invited Kay to teach the Bible in her lovely Atlanta antebellum home.

Grace was a great encourager for Kay. Grace mentored her and encouraged Kay in her ministry's infancy. Grace's home was filled to the brim with people when Kay came to teach. An off-duty policeman was needed to keep the traffic under control. Finally, the city asked Mrs. Kinser to move the Bible study to a church, and she gracefully did.

I am convinced that God loves to use homes for ministry. In the confines of a home, a ministry can be more personal. The home reflects the owner's love of God. I believe that some of these large estate homes were conceived with this idea in mind. Take what God has given you and use it for His glory!

Consider starting this kind of outreach in your town. Find a facilitator and ask a group of women to come study the Bible. Be creative! Choose a topic or have a book study. There are many studies available today. Ask your Christian bookstores to suggest a study for you. Use your home as Esther did. She saw the opportunity to do God's work right there in the palace.

Queen Esther's Reflection

Make your home a palace, a place for the King to reside. Remember that you are called to transact royal business. Use your gifts and talents to refresh others. Be a way station for weary travelers. Allow the fragrance of grace and hospitality to come forth from you as well as your home.

Study Guide

1. Ask God to show you how to transform your home.

2. Prepare each room for comfort and ministry.

3. Name five things that you know are essentials for creating an oasis.

4. What are you expecting God to teach you through Esther's hospitality?

5. What are the most refreshing areas of your home?

6. What is the most important lesson for you in this chapter?

CHAPTER 7

Spirit of the Home . . . Warm Hospitality

Glimpses of Grace
"Do you want to stand out? Be a servant."
—Matthew 23:11 *(The Message)*

W HEN I speak of hospitality, I'm speaking with a southern accent. That statement can conjure up a lot of smiles—y'alls and drawls. This means that manners and graces are expected. If you had a southern mother, grandmother, or aunt, you know what I mean. To love, hug, and greet people is just part of the southern culture. We southerners are taught from generation to generation to welcome people into our world with love, respect, and social grace. A warm welcome is the expectation, not the exception. This is what people love about the South.

The saying "You never get a second chance to make a first impression" is so true. A warm welcome goes a long way! It is the introduction to who you are. Within the first two seconds of meeting you, others form an opinion of who you are. How you look, carry yourself, and most of all what you say matters very much! When you say the wrong thing or do the wrong thing it can take years to undo or make up for this misstep. This is why being aware of how people see you, allowing yourself to come under discipline, and to be able to give a warm greeting is essential for a successful life. Esther knew this. She excelled at doing this. I am confident that palace protocol benefited her in this area!

What is needed for a warm welcome? Look no further than Galatians 5:22–23. Here we find the roster of the fruit of the Spirit—love, joy, peace, longsuffering, kindness, goodness, faithfulness, gentleness, and last, but not least, self-control.

The Foyer

The interior designer in me would tell you that the foyer of your home introduces your home to guests and piques their interest in the rest of the house. It is the beginning of the painter's palette. What you introduce in this room will be carried forth throughout the home. In the same way, when someone meets you, they instantly form an opinion of who you are. How you look and what you say are like a foyer of you!

Foyer meetings are first impressions; making a good one is biblical. We as believers should aim to be kind, hospitable, and loving. These are our colors and fabrics. The women in my family modeled this to me. If you did not experience this kind of training as a child or young adult, you can receive it now. It is never too late.

Hospitality

In researching for this book, I found many Scriptures about hospitality. Christian living is all about this subject: loving others and serving them. Jesus Christ is our model for this. He served so well that He gave His life for us to be able to have an eternal life with Him—the ultimate hospitality!

There are many models of grace and hospitality in Scripture. Lydia used her gifts of hospitality to advance Paul's ministry and the gospel. Then there are Mary and Martha, and the Proverbs 31 woman of many hats. These women of faith knew how to serve. They invited people into their home sanctuaries to hear the Lord. We know women who have the incredible gift of making people welcome hospitably and with grace. Whether they are our mothers or grandmothers or just friends, we know them.

When we become Christians, we get a "double hospitality anointing." Christians show hospitality like no other people in the world. When you mix a natural talent with a spirit-filled, inspired gifting you really get the full dose! I see this all over the country when I speak!

I am often hosted in private homes when I am away speaking. Every comfort is provided; every need is met; every special touch is placed at my fingertips; and I appreciate it. I see the love and preparation that has been extended to me. This is love in action—hospitality at its finest.

Memories flood over me from my childhood, a fondness for both of my grandmothers. They were both women of great hospitality. My paternal grandmother was a strict Southern Baptist. She was a no-nonsense, Bible-teaching and believing woman of God. She knew the Word of God. She was serious about respect and responsibility. She was a wise, very disciplined, capable woman. As a child, I saw her as too strict and too determined to make me read and study. Oh, how I would love to have her helping me edit these books! I remember her preparing for Woman's Missionary Union meetings. She would polish the silver, set flowers on the table, and prepare delicious food. This was her greatest joy. Serving the Lord made her happy, it put a twinkle in her eye! She was serious about spreading the gospel.

My maternal grandmother, a Methodist, lived in Charleston, South Carolina. She had an incredible ability to love. Her name should have been Grace. Grandmother Winnie made everyone feel so important. She listened to everything a person said—at least she did this with *me*. She gave me time and place. I loved that. Her gift was to put her arms around me, love me, and feed me. God brought me into the world and deposited me in a family of grace. I never knew anything different.

Hospitality was extended in my childhood home. Born into a political family, I was exposed to a lot of people of different cultures and socioeconomic differences. This has served me well in my adult life. Politics has a tarnished image, but there is a good side. My parents had a genuine love of people. They both had the gift of hospitality and enjoyed helping people. They often hosted events in our home and even took in strangers.

Unbelievable Hospitality!

In their later years, my parents often dined out in the evenings. Our beloved Clara, the family cook, was getting older, and my parents wanted Clara to have early afternoons off.

Our small hometown of Orangeburg, South Carolina, had a wonderful restaurant called Berry's on the Hill. This dining facility was well known by travelers coming from the North going to Miami on Highway 301. Often, people would call an hour before to make sure they were expected—and to ask to have the frozen coconut pie defrosted a little!

Daddy would drop Mother off at Berry's, and then go by the post office to get his last mail drop. Mother would go ahead and order for them. When people were there that were not locals, Mother would introduce herself. She felt it her obligation to do this as the senator's wife, and she felt that it was gracious southern hospitality.

One particular evening mother was seated next to an older couple. In the conversation, they told her that they had been married earlier that day and were on their honeymoon. Mother asked where they were planning to spend the night. The husband said that he was going to try to get a room in Columbia, the nearest large town. He had tried to get a room in Orangeburg, but it seemed that there was not a room available. Without hesitation, my mother invited them to spend the night at her house. They were speechless.

When my father returned, Mother introduced him to the newlyweds. "Where are you staying?" Daddy asked the couple. The man tensed up, but told him the same thing that he had told Mother.

"They're having the ACC basketball championships there. You won't find a room in town. Why don't you come spend the night with us?" Daddy blurted out.

Daddy picked up the man's check. "Come on and follow me." My father expected people to do what he suggested. A man of authority, he walked out the restaurant leading the way to their home. I had just finished redecorating the master bedroom. During the painting and repair, my parents had moved into the guest room. Daddy liked it there. It was away from the telephone, off in one of the wings, and very private.

Upon walking into the beautiful master bedroom, Mother said in her Low Country drawl, "Now, this is where we keep all our brides and grooms." The couple exchanged glances and said good-night to her. Then mother heard them set the lock.

Willbrook, my parents' home, looks like the mansion Tara from *Gone with the Wind*, with huge columns and wrought-iron stair railings. These newlyweds were brought into a world of great beauty: French crystal chandeliers, ancestral portraits, antique period pieces, a master suite, dressing rooms larger than most bedrooms. A long dressing table with a marble top, silver brushes, and a collection of perfume bottles adorned the master suite. This bride and groom entered a fabulous world—high ceilings, pale petal-pink walls, a boudoir layered with beauty and comfort. It's what Esther must have felt like walking into the palace: creams and perfumes, lotions, crystal chandeliers everywhere, and even monogrammed towels.

Hospitality in Turbulent Times

As we move into more turbulent times, homes will become key places of refuge. A different kind of hospitality will be needed. As the world becomes more dangerous, people will be called upon to open their homes to people in ministry. These homes will be centered around prayer and relationship. God will certainly give His people discernment.

Families may open their homes even for a sandwich, drink of water, or a safe place for those sent their way. In the same manner, women will be mentoring younger women. Take a good look at your home, your talents, and the whole picture. See how God is going to use you.

Take a closer look at Esther's hospitality. When she invited Haman, she was planning to extend hospitality to a person who hated God and the Jews. She knew when to issue the invitation and who needed to be on the guest list. Her house was in order. Mordecai had the plan. Esther was the thin line that would hold Israel together at this place in time. It all depended on one dinner party—excuse me, two dinner parties!

Creativity and Ways to Entertain

Today's woman uses her home for more than family time; she opens her doors to ministry and love. You don't like to entertain the same way twice? Neither do I. If you are a creative hostess, you like to mix it up! From all accounts Esther threw the best parties in Persia. Esther would say, "Keep your guests guessing. Never do it the same way twice." This is the reason her dinner parties were legendary. Her entertaining plans had other meanings. I believe she captivated her guests. Her enemy, Haman, coveted her invitation.

Making people feel at home in your house is one of the grace gifts that come from a heart of love and giving. I believe that providing for ministry in this manner is pleasing to God. He can use you in this way for His own purposes. This is strategic entertaining, and it's possible you may entertain angels in this way. You can make all kinds of things happen! Through hospitality you might:

- make important private meetings possible;
- facilitate healing for a sick person;
- help issue a call to a budding leader;
- make others aware of necessary timing;
- serve as God's emissary;
- introduce people to each other—networking for God.

You never know who God is placing in front of you—door-openers, mentors, or part of God's chain of command. They were positioned by the Lord to take my ministry to a certain level or certain place. Do it with a pure heart, but expect God to be present.

When you love the Lord, your playground and playmates change. Those with whom you had little in common now become fascinating people. You realize the "in crowd" is made up of those directed to you by the Lord. Your sphere of influence and friends looks like the United Nations.

Bountiful Hostess

Esther, a seasoned woman with grace and knowledge, knew how to honor her guests. She innately understood the bigger picture—what they liked, how to present it, who the other guests should be, how to treat and introduce them. Bountiful women are prepared women. They are not just hostesses for a few events; they are the event. They understand biblical hospitality.

Women of hospitality represent the abundant, ample, plenteous, plentiful, generous gift of providing. What I am talking about is more than food; it is bounty of the Spirit and the seasoning for the occasion. These women become the flavoring. The food and accompaniment become secondary. They have pulled out their hospitality chests—more than flowers, more than menu, more than details. These favored women are purposed and focused on what they need and how to provide. They actually spill over with the gift of love through hospitality. My mother is one of these women—born to host.

Esther is a biblical example of a woman of hospitality. She knew when to come, when to speak, and when to strike. We learn from the Esthers of this world to become refined, prepared, and ready. By being available for kingdom event planning, you are able to do things others do not even see. Get your houses in order. Make your home a palace. Get ready for the next level of grace God has waiting for you.

I believe that we are coming to a time when we will open our homes to many people with a variety of situations. We may take in friends for a season or people traveling and relocating. These times will call for prophet chambers to be filled with people of ministry. If you have one such room, get it ready for God's people to use.

QUEEN ESTHER'S REFLECTION

Open up your home to prayer and ministry. Trust God with the plans and purposes of your life. Be a woman of great hospitality. Prepare for a revival in you! Do not fear for tomorrow. Live today. This day alone is what we have been promised.

Study Guide

1. Give God permission to work on your fear of hospitality.

2. Make a list of all the people that you need to invite to your home.

3. Take inventory of your entertaining chest. What do you need to add?

4. Plan a small party in honor of a friend.

5. Write letters to friends who mean a lot to you.

6. Say thank you to your parents. Say it in as many ways as you can.

CHAPTER 8

A Loving Marriage

Glimpses of Grace

"An excellent wife is the crown of her husband, but she who shames him is like rottenness in his bones."
—Proverbs 12:4 (NASB)

MY JOURNEY in love has taught me many things. First, like Esther, I have learned by being mentored. These teachings have taught me much about men. I want to share what I know. I have had the honor and pleasure of speaking to thousands of women all over the US. I love being able to go into places where I can speak love and life into marriages. Because my life was so radically changed, and I was given a second chance at love, I feel empowered to go and speak. I am also the coauthor, with Susan Wales, of two volumes of *A Match Made in Heaven*. These books are short stories of successful marriages.

Men have two basic needs—to be loved and to be respected. The first need is basically through intimacy in sexual relations. They want this love from their wives. It is high on their list of needs. The second need is to have the respect of their wives. If this respect is not given, they will seek it elsewhere. This is what destroyed the king's marriage to Vashti. She publicly disrespected her husband. When I read the Book of Esther, I saw Vashti's problem. Whether or not she had the right to refuse to be a display for her husband, there was a higher spiritual situation going on. Vashti broke one of the cardinal rules of marriage—she disrespected her husband.

Below I have listed my top ten nonnegotiables that I share with women. These are the things that you must pay attention to in order to have a loving marriage. Take a serious look at what I am suggesting. Implement these rules into your lives and marriage and see what a difference this will make.

Top Ten Nonnegotiables in Marriage

1. **Intimacy.** Be intimate with him. God gave sexual intimacy as a gift for marriage. Sexual intimacy was meant to empower the man. The same enzymes are used in sex as those used when armies go forth to conquer. Do not neglect this area of your marriage.

2. **Respect him.** The number two need of a husband is respect. If a man does not get the respect of his wife, then the marriage will not last. No whining. No criticizing. No nagging. No bossing and running the show. Allow him to choose. You are not his mother.

3. **Never correct** your husband in public. Do not use sarcasm. Sarcasm is the inability to communicate. Watch your tone. An overbearing nature is not feminine. Watch your tongue. An overbearing spirit can lead to disaster.

4. **Listen to him.** Perfect the art of listening. Do you want to shut him down or encourage him? Respond in love. Ask yourself, *Am I being soft?* Listen for what bothers him about you. He will be repeating it to you time after time . . . hear it and change. A smart woman listens.

5. **Thank him.** Have a grateful heart. Speak it out. Say, "Thank you for this house." Men adore being thanked. Look for things to thank him for daily and say them. A grateful woman will be beloved by her husband.

6. **Know him.** Find out his love language (see Gary Chapman's *The Five Love Languages* book) and personality type (see Tim LaHaye's *The Spirit-Controlled Temperament* book). A wise woman knows her husband.

7. **Serve him, and allow him to serve you.** Compliment him when he opens the door for you; thank him for preparing a beverage for you. Express gratitude to him when he serves you breakfast in bed. Don't let him feel like you don't need him. Ask for help.

8. **Pray together.** Have a specific time of prayer for each other for wisdom and direction. Ask him to pray for your needs. Ask him to lay hands on you and pray for you. He will love this. Start small and grow together. Keep a prayer journal.

9. **Make time for fun.** Develop intimacy with God first, then with your husband. Take time to know him. Do not neglect this opportunity to love your husband.

Make him feel loved and important. Go to ball games with him if he likes that . . . or fishing . . . find some things in common that you both will enjoy . . . broaden your scope . . . be his friend. Give him space and your attention.

10. **Fight for your man!** If someone comes against your husband, protect him. Do not allow your children to say anything against him. Do not gossip to your friends about your husband. Honor him in everything that you say and do. Let him know that you are a fighting woman . . . for him!

Alert!

My friend's husband was unfaithful. He was well known in his community. The other woman went under the radar screen. She was more than 15 years older than he, not very attractive, and not an obvious threat to anyone's husband. My friend was clueless and trusting. The other woman was a businesswoman, a member of their church, and needed a lot of spiritual advice.

Who would think? Because the other woman was an older woman who saw the special abilities of this man, the relationship went unnoticed. It seemed like a great friendship. My friend even encouraged her husband to get involved in this woman's business! Watch out for disguised Jezebels. Make your husband a top priority! Ask God to protect your marriage.

More Advice

1. Get those best friends out of the house when your husband comes home.
2. Watch out for needy women around your husband.
3. Pay attention to the sounds in your home . . . turn off the TV and play lovely music.
3. Keep your radar up and going.
4. Love your husband . . . affirm him.
5. And, oh, those *Little House on the Prairie* nightgowns— cut them up, especially the nightgowns that have four or more yards of fabric in them. Use them for dust cloths. Do not wear them around your husband! Well, only if the heat goes off, and you have to have them to survive!
6. Perfume yourself. Follow Esther's regime. Wear the fragrance he likes or compliments. Wear his favorite color. Do you even know his favorite color?
7. Please do not criticize his mother. Bite your tongue if you have to. A man will defend his mother even if she is a raging lunatic. Do not point out her bad ways. He knows.

Some godly words that heal and restore marriages

I love you . . . I am sorry . . . Thank you . . . You are awesome!
Where would I be without you?
You are the most wonderful husband in the world!
You sure look mighty handsome today!
*I see Jesus in you (*if you do)*!*

Some "Home" Tips

1. Make your husband your number one priority!

    a. Add some loving touches . . . frame some pictures of him as a child.

    b. Tell him something sweet that he has done lately.

    c. Ask him what you can do to help him.

    d. Do something to help him organize his things.

2. Keep your house clean and straight.
No draping clothes over chairs. For some this is hard, so it is a sacrifice.

3. Remember to play soft restful music.
Soothe frayed nerves and set a relaxing atmosphere at night and at bedtime. Purchase a CD player for the bedside table. Go to sleep listening to soft instrumental music.

4. Do little things that your husband likes.
Bring joy into his life and day! Serve his favorite food. Plant his favorite flowers. Add little love touches throughout your home. John places a flower on my pillow, and I write love notes for him!

5. Find some time each night to listen to your husband's day. Do not advise or fix him. If he asks, give your opinion . . . but only when asked!

Ann Platz's Recommended Reading List on Marriage:
1. *The Five Love Languages*, by Gary Chapman

2. *His Needs/Her Needs,* by Willard Harley
3. *The Spirit-Controlled Temperament,* by Tim LaHaye
4. *The Power of a Praying Wife,* by Stormie O'Martian
5. *A Match Made in Heaven,* vols. 1 and 2, by Ann Platz and Susan Wales
6. Wives*: For Better or for Best,* by Gary Smalley
7. Husbands*: If He Only Knew,* by Gary Smalley

Just as respect is vital to a marriage relationship, so is praise. I have observed married women who praise their spouses and others who curse their husbands. There is a marked difference in these marriages. Women who rule their husbands are out of order. It will not be long before those men are looking for a way out, either by shutting down or ignoring their wives. Esther will tell you this one thing, "Your tongue will bring forth what your heart feels about your husband. So be careful what you say."

If we could bottle humility as a fragrance, I would purchase gallons of this scent. It would be my fragrance of choice. Humility is a virtue that is the essence of a true godly woman. It comes from living a lifestyle of grace. Humility's aroma in a woman is irresistible to a man. Its bouquet smells of respect, honor, love, patience, goodness, joy, gentleness, and virtue. This was Esther's fragrance. Her beauty contest opponents did not stand a chance!

In honoring her husband, Esther poured love into him. He loved her—Scripture said so. Love's powerful control over our emotions caused this husband to trust his wife. The king wanted to give to her and provide for her. As she honored him, he gave. God intended this to be a love match.

Because Esther honored her husband, she was placed in position to ask for whatever she needed. This was the setup of the Lord!

Esther's ability to overlook the palace scene and the party that lasted for months was key to her success as a potential wife. She became obedient to the call of God on her life. This became her focus. Her marriage possibility was her goal. Without this relationship, she would not be able to have the godly influence that she needed. She disciplined herself to do the beauty routines, exercise, and whatever else she had to do. She looked to the goal that was set before her, took instructions, and obeyed her mentor. She submitted and committed. This is a strong godly message to today's young women.

Submitting to One Another

Esther discovered the fine art of submitting through listening. This was certainly pleasing to the king after enduring a rebellious wife who refused to come when he commanded her presence. Esther's humble nature and her eagerness to listen surely blessed this king's heart. Her ability to submit to her husband in every way was refreshing after his experience with Vashti's disobedience.

In Titus 2:3–5, older women are admonished to teach younger women to love their husbands and children and to live a sober, clean life, being keepers of their homes and being kind and obedient to their husbands. As husbands and wives submit to one another, the marriage becomes secure in the Lord.

Knowing Him

A wife needs the ability to know her husband intimately. She needs to *know* his ways. She needs to know what makes him happy, as well as what makes him furious. A wise woman does not do things that cause her spouse to get upset. She builds her marriage; she does not tear it down.

As his partner and mate, a Christian woman has the blessing of ministering to her husband when he needs prayer. She speaks hope and blessing into his life. She reminds him of the things that God has done for them in the past. She also can comfort him like no other person can. I know my husband has been my greatest comfort in times of great need. He would pray for hours for me when I was grieving over the loss of my only sister, even standing over me during the night in prayer for peace.

A wise women's desire to comfort and love her man will set in motion a level of trust and security that the enemy cannot come against. A woman of wisdom will encourage her husband in every way. She will speak words of comfort and not words of complaint. As she builds her marriage, she builds her home and family legacy. Give advice when asked. Do not preach to your husbands.

A good wife is a blessing to a man. He will love her and do for her as he feels her love and respect. Remember that blessings and cursing can come from the same lips. Choose blessings. Esther was a comfort for her husband. She desired to please him.

Outside the Palace

Imagine this: Esther is in the outer court, ready to come before her husband, the king. He has not called for her. Entering without a summons from the king carried a penalty of death, if the king chose this form of punishment. So when Esther chose to enter the king's presence to plead for her life and the lives of her people, it was a dangerous move. Her boldness was needed. The events of the day caused her to realize that the time to go in was now. If the king raised the scepter, she would be safe.

I remember what it felt like to be in the outer court and not inside the palace. This was my feeling when I was struggling after my divorce. I wanted to feel loved. I desired for my life to have purpose. My security and dreams were shattered. My marriage had failed. I felt very far away from God. I did not know how to reach Him. I prayed, but felt nothing. I sat in church with tears streaming down my cheeks. I was in extreme depression and grief. I did not understand that this too would pass. All I knew was that I was miserable. I wanted desperately to be comforted.

God will allow you to come to the end of yourself. He did this with me. I had married out of the will of God. I had planned my life as I wanted it to be. I had asked Him to stamp my plans as one would stamp a passport. I wanted to go here and there. I never took drugs or abused alcohol, but I was willful. I wanted to do what I wanted to do. After all, it was the 1960s, and people were crazy. Religion was being ridiculed. The world was in rebellion. All these ideas and plans had taken me far away from whom I was and where I was really supposed to be. Really, they had taken me in the opposite direction. My rebellion seemed miniscule, but in the eyes of God, I was a sinner.

Then my life came crashing down around me. I came full circle, and I was able to be in the place where God would raise His scepter. I was allowed to come home to Him. I would go into His courts freely as a daughter. I do not know why it took me so long to figure this out. Thank goodness, I did get it all straight in my mind and heart!

QUEEN ESTHER'S REFLECTION

Allow the Lord to teach you about covenant marriage. The spiritual disciplines of marriage are there to cover and protect you, not place you under bondage. Place your trust in the Word of God.

Study Guide

1. Ask God to reveal to you His truths about the commitment of marriage.

2. Make a list of five couples that you know who have great marriages. What do they do that others do not?

3. Name five things that you know are essentials for a good marriage.

A Loving Marriage

4. What are you expecting God to teach you through Esther's royal marriage?

5. Name five traits of a godly wife that Esther exhibited.

6. What traits of Esther's marriage do you want to apply to your life?

CHAPTER 9

When Marriage Is Difficult

Glimpses of Grace

*"But seek first the kingdom of God and His righteous-
ness, and all these things shall be added to you."*
—Matthew 6:33

ESTHER WAS not a woman without difficulties. First
of all, her husband was somewhat difficult. Today's
counselors would label him excessive and abusive, yet God
did not give her a green light to protest being involved with
him. Instead, the plan of God was a covert action to protect
His people through her. She followed a higher plan on a
higher plane.

God would not let her go any direction other than His
destiny for the nation of Israel. It was bigger than marriage.
It was bigger than if He had split everyone in the palace in

half. God's plan defied counseling and human reasoning. It defied what seemed to be wisdom. It defied all human logic! Who in the world would want a husband who entertained his friends for 180 days straight or chose a wife from a line of beauty contestants? No woman I know!

I am not saying that if you are under an abusive husband God is necessarily saying for you to stay there and be abused. Just know when to go! There are times when God will say . . . *You stay and allow Me to do the huge thing that no one else can do!* Then other times God says, *Go!*

Man cannot understand the realm in which God exists. When the situation is huge, complicated, and confusing, you can get deterred. But don't listen to those who will send you down rabbit trails . . . stay focused.

Picture a modern-day Esther. She is focused, turning away phone calls, turning down invitations for the normal things of the day to stay tuned to God. She could not afford to miss the direction of God— in any way. She is alerted to watch for the signs—His signal that the order of her day has changed.

I used to come unglued when someone canceled an appointment with me on the day of the scheduled meeting. I do not know why, but it irritated me tremendously, especially if it was for an unimportant reason. I guess I thought that it meant they lacked respect for me. God began to deal with me about this. He began to show me that He was alerting me to some divine appointments. If I would loosen up, He would do His work in that area. Then it began to happen. Now it has become almost fun to watch what God is allowing to come forward in my life.

Esther had an unusual ability to wait and trust God. She sure had a lot more of this virtue than I did. Her priorities were so aligned with God that she was freed up to let her beauty be used for the glory of God. She was seeking first the kingdom of heaven and all the rest was being added. After all, that's what makes a woman beautiful anyway.

If Esther were at lunch today with divorced women—say three women who were considering divorce—she would say, "Don't you leave until you have tried every means of reconciliation, turned over every stone, and until God Himself gives you a green light—that is something that only YOU will know! Not even a majority vote from friends and family will overrule God's guidance for you."

My first husband and I spent a year in counseling. Each visit brought no reconciliation—no move forward. Tired of trying to make a marriage work, after a year of struggle, he packed up and left after a simple verbal encounter on a Saturday morning. Later I discovered that he was involved with another woman and this was the reason that he would not do any work toward reconciling our fragile marriage. I was trying to solve a problem not realizing that it was not going to be solved the way I thought.

Many women are in the same situation as I found myself. Years later, after I gained much more maturity, I can see that God was releasing me that day. I felt the release and did not know what to call it. It was the protection of my Lord.

I know that as I write about this subject there will be many women with troubled marriages reading this book. Frustrated and heartbroken over the loss of the commitment that you gave the Lord, God will speak to you individually about your situations. I do not recommend divorce. It is a last resort. And just as He released me, He will indeed direct you as to what you should do. This I promise!

If Esther were with us for breakfast at my favorite Atlanta restaurant, the OK Café, she would say to women who are having marital difficulties: "Girls, this is where the rubber meets the road; be a wise woman!"

1. **Go straight to God.**
2. **Pray and fast.** This is not optional. When your marriage is at stake, the devil is coming at the very core of your life. Fight back with spiritual warfare.
3. **Seek godly counsel**. Talk with people who are more concerned about what God would have you do than popular psychology or personal opinion.
4. **Ask mentors and people of integrity to pray with you.** It is important to surround yourself with these godly people. If they are not currently in your life, ask God to bring them into your life. He will!
5. **Look to the future.** God has something so much bigger than what you can see at that point, or what you think you want and need. Satan wants you trapped and compromised. God has a great future for you!

Esther had to die to everything she had hoped, prayed for, or imagined, to do this kingdom work. This is usually the test. God gives you a choice to be great for Him.

I was asked to speak to a lovely group of women in New Orleans—just a few months after the devastating hurricane disasters. I shared that I had endured my own Katrina many years earlier through a divorce. Mine did not come with water and floods, but it came with the same gale force to destroy me, my children, and my home. With God's redeeming help I not only survived, I became whole through the experience. That season caused me to spiritually wake up and fully give my life to the Lord. I encouraged them to trust God with the details. I was sure that He would rebuild my life greater than before. After all, it is His nature to do so.

A few years ago, I went to speak in another city. Little did I know, but it was an Esther assignment. One of my spiritual daughters invited me to speak at a conference in her city. I knew her situation with her marriage was not good—really disastrous. It was almost gone. There was another woman involved. I had counseled my friend to stay and pray—to watch the deliverance of God. I was certain that God would intervene and restore my friend's hopes and dreams.

When I arrived at her home, I saw the Haman setup. God connected some dots right there for me to see. The gallows was built. This was figuratively, but spiritually true. Evil was waiting to destroy this woman. Satan wanted this place. A Jezebel was in place to take it.

I thought to myself . . . *Oh, no! Not on my watch!* I got mad—a righteous anger! All I could see all over my spiritual daughter's life was death—death of her marriage, death of her dreams, death of her ministry, and death to everything else. I could hear the enemy whispering to her . . . *Put the noose around your neck and die.*

From God's point of view, He wanted a death all right—death to everything in the flesh that tells you to bail out. Dying to self will bring about God's purposes and plans every time. God's net is wider. He fishes in deeper waters. He wants to catch all—not only the victim, but also the sinner. I told my daughter, "Watch how God is going to do this." I was sure that we were going to see a miracle.

The Holy Spirit began to release an anointing of love to the women in that conference. He began to heal, restore, and bring life to lost dreams and hopelessness. I take no credit for what happened because it was way out of my ability to do anything like this, but God got hold of the mistress. He began to work a deep work within her.

Months before, my spiritual daughter had prayed, surrendered this situation to God, and made herself available to be used by God for this woman's healing and restoration. This was the spiritual setup for what took place at the conference.

At the conference, I called for a healing line for those who wanted to be all that God wanted them to be. I prayed over each woman, for them to be set free from the bondage that had ensnared them. When the fallen woman stood before me, I embraced her. I could see the desire for repentance in her face. I could hear her cry. I knew that it was over—over in the spiritual realm. God had broken through, as only He can do. That night He touched her broken heart.

All of us stand before God as sinners needing a Savior. Just as this woman was forgiven, so can we be given the same blessing. What God wants to create is a tapestry through you— a thing of beauty. As prophets of old told of hope, so does the person today who is yielded to God.

On Watch in the Workplace

Today's working women face many pitfalls because of male-female relationships at work. When your male boss wants to discuss his troubled marriage with you, it is always a trap. Rather than you becoming the counselor, guide him to get the help for himself and his wife from a professional. This keeps you out of the possible setup. Say out loud, "If you need to talk about trouble in your marriage, talk to a counselor. I will not be able to listen to that topic." You will have to stand firm in setting this limit. The problem will come up again, and again, until he gets it. Being the listening ear, the understanding heart, the encourager, is always a huge trap! Women have the need to help, nurture, and make everything OK. Needy men will gravitate to this kind of woman. This is why trying to counsel in this kind of situation is so dangerous—meeting his needs, helping him, pulling you into being a part of the answer.

A friend tells of how she was lured into a five-year affair. Mary got personally involved with her boss. He said that his wife was cold toward him. He also told that the wife had some form of mental illness. He said he was staying with her because of the family, but that the love was gone.

Mary foolishly walked right into the trap that was set. Before long she was taking trips with him. Desperate to be with him, she compromised her faith, her values, and her life. She drifted away from her friends and family. She became isolated, waiting for him to call.

Desperate, she decided to call a psychic! What she did was call the devil.

The psychic told her things about her father and grand-father that were true. She believed everything the psychic told her. Mary's lover knew her grandfather. She believed that the man she was in love with was destined to be her husband. The relationship lasted five years. Going to that psychic cost her ten years of her life—the five years in it and five years to come out of it. This was an expensive mistake!

Mary got desperate. She went to three psychiatrists try-ing to come out of this web of deception. They told her to look inward. She was never held accountable for her sinful actions.

A Campus Crusade speaker came to town. A good friend invited Mary to hear him speak. It was as simple as the speaker giving a basic salvation message. He said that we are all sinners and we need a Savior. Jesus Christ came to redeem us from our sins.

God showed Mary the problem was that she was a sin-ner! Simple as that. That night she prayed to receive the Lord Jesus as her Savior and Redeemer. She asked to be forgiven so that she could receive healing from the wrong relationship.

"I was born again tonight!" Mary told her lover. The lover reacted and told her that she was rejecting him. He left. He knew it was over—and it was over!

Women, this is the final word on marriage difficulties: There are a million ways to go wrong, and only one sure way to go right—and it's Esther's way. Trust in the Lord. Seek His guidance. Follow the path God lays out for you, whatever it is.

QUEEN ESTHER'S REFLECTION

Ask for God's guidance in the difficulties of your marriage, whether they be small and simple or huge and intimidating. Let God remind you that neither partner in your marriage is perfect, and that both are deeply loved by Him!

Study Guide

1. What are the ways that you typically deal with difficulties in your marriage? Have those ways been successful for the marriage?

2. If you and your husband needed marital advice or counseling, do you have a trusted mentor you can call? If not, pray to the Lord to provide you with a guide, someone who will be an advocate for your marriage and for both you and your husband.

3. Do you think of your marriage mainly in terms of how you feel about it currently? Think about what larger purpose God might have for you in your marriage.

4. What can you learn from Esther about dealing with marital difficulties?

Part Three

Queen Esther's Reflection

"I am a little pencil in the hand of a writing God who is sending a love letter to the world."

—Mother Teresa

CHAPTER 10

Woman of Grace in the Marketplace

Glimpses of Grace

"Eye hath not seen, nor ear heard, nor have entered into the heart of man, the things which God hath prepared for those who love him."

—1 Corinthians 2:9

W HEN ESTHER became queen of Persia, the palace became her workplace as well as her home. She was a successful woman as much because of her mastery of palace politics and court relationships as her beauty. Esther would certainly sympathize with working women of today, and she would have a lot to teach them! Women of today face an immense set of challenges.

Spiritual darkness, greed, and ungodliness are rampant in corporate America. Extremely devious setups are requiring that Christians apply whatever spiritual warfare is necessary. People in authority are doing surveillance by tapping phone conversations, listening in on private conversations, and even hiring people to come in the company to see where the loyalties lie.

Pride and arrogance are also at an all-time high. Where is the service? Where are the servant hearts? Leadership has become aggressive and competitive. People advance by positioning themselves and taking credit for things that they have not done. Integrity is at an all-time low.

In a work structure, you can often find a Haman in authority. If you do not bow to this person, watch out! Hamans promote the ones they can control. If you keep your integrity, refuse to bow, won't allow yourself to be controlled, then you become marked.

Look at what is happening today. Large corporations are falling because of the Hamans in charge. They put people of no integrity or the ones who will compromise in places of authority. They lie, cheat the stockholders, and have not an ounce of regret or repentance. These same people steal these companies blind, and refuse to admit that they do anything wrong. These executives put a board of directors in place who will compromise. Read about it in the newspapers.

What is even worse is when people do this and don't even see that it is wrong and sinful. Who do they think that they are fooling? After all, they will reap what they have sown. The world operates in the daytime, but God awakens His saints in the night to dream—and show where the enemy is.

No wonder people's lives are falling apart. Look at the devastation of some of the huge corporations, broken marriages, and ministries that are in trouble. What went wrong? It begins with compromising, being legally correct but morally wrong, and forming a circle and web of deception.

When a Haman is leading, you'd best watch out. Those who support the Haman agenda are highly favored. Those who will resist the Hamans will be marked. But read the rest of the story, as Paul Harvey says. Haman was hanged on his own gallows. He fell into the pit he dug for his marked target; this is a "reap what you sow" ending! Although it is difficult when you are in this kind of situation, it is possible to remain a godly person.

When we want to walk in God's will, we must be careful not to miss what our Mordecai mentors say to us—especially to point out any blind spots. We need these people who keep us walking on dead center. So much is at stake in so many cases. For example, in churches where a pastor gets into sin, we need to pray for him. And pray for a bold Mordecai to come into his life—a person equipped with love and mercy to minister wholeness and reconciliation.

Setting a Standard in the Marketplace

There are some things that you can do that will greatly aid you in preparing for each day at work. I have listed four things that I think will turn your perspective around.

1. **Stay in the Word.** Have personal devotions every day for 30 minutes.

2. **Have an agenda.** Make a plan for each day. Make it out the night before.

3. **Stay respectful of others.** Do not try to control or change people! They will resent this.

4. **Make your boss look good.** Even if he is not a Christian, he is your leader. Look for his leadership qualification. If he is not qualified for the job, try to help him. The Lord will bless you. If you hear people talking about him behind his back, try to stop this. He may be going through a very hard time.

Also when you have a Haman, like Esther did, this person will cause you to think on your feet. Sometimes this kind of person is the sandpaper that helps us smooth out our rough edges. This is exactly what Esther did. She held back and waited for the message to go forward.

We can create a bad situation by being hasty. What if Esther had gone to the king, told on Haman, and demanded such and such? The king could have said, "You do not know what you're talking about." He would have defended his man. Instead, she planned the banquet and brought the king aboard. The timing is so important.

Workplace Wisdom

My friend Karen Finley, even after a successful corporate career, wants to do more. She has been a speaker for many years in corporate situations. Now she wants to use her speaking skills to give back, open doors for others, and share her story of how she charted the waters of her career. She is aware that a speaker can reach a lot of people from a platform. Karen also wants to use her home more for ministry, Bible studies, and prayer groups. Although she has done this in the past, she is ready for more ministries.

Karen has seen the marketplace open up for women over the years. There has been such a big increase in women coming into the workplace. She was the first female sales representative with the Dale Carnegie organization in the 1960s. Back then, women who worked were either secretaries, nurses, or teachers. Corporations could not see that a woman could possibly do what a man did.

Back in those days, clients would ask if a saleswoman doing outside sales was the secretary. When the saleswoman said no, the client would say, "Bring back a man so I can relate to that person." Karen would nicely say, "I'm the representative, may I talk with you?" The change was very hard for many clients.

Esther would have wisdom for marketplace situations. I believe that she would say, "Go for it, girl—aim high!" She would like to see women more involved in leadership roles because of their discernment and decision-making abilities. And don't leave out their ability to do multiple tasks! She would also say to venture out and have more compassion, more sensitivity, and more personal impact. This is one of the largest areas that Karen is called to help correct. Most of the managers that Karen works with need help in: understanding; patience; compassion; good timing; and listening skills.

Esther showed that she had a strong business sense. She did not jump to conclusions, rather she gathered all the information, had a plan, and thought it through. She waited to present her plan—perfect timing. Esther knew God would bring her forward in His timing!

Planting in Season

Timing is everything. Knowing the right time to plant, sow, and harvest. This will mean the difference in success or failure. While my friend Karen had the opportunity to teach in Germany, she traveled in 35 countries. This opportunity gave her insight as to how other people live, and especially the differences in the cultures. Then, when she worked for 20 years with the employment service organization Norrell Corporation, she traveled in a five-state region. This career gave her independence. Having had the Dale Carnegie background certainly helped paved the way to do what she is doing today. She is now a management consultant with BellSouth.

"You always go through adversity with bosses," Karen said. "It is part of the challenge of working. Some people are very complicated. You must understand this and not allow them to take you off on rabbit trails. You have to look where you're going and not let someone steal your joy and your plans. It is wise to know that some people are there to be sandpaper in your life. They will help you be the person that God wants you to be. Sometimes it seems unbearable, but the Lord helps you through those times of adversity.

"Then there are times when you need to make a change. You will know when it is time to go. You will feel the release of the Lord. When a door is closed there is a window open someplace. The Lord will help you see what He has out there for you. Too many times we stand still when we need to move into a different place. For example, when the door was closed at Norrell, God led me to form my own consulting business. Norrell was one of my first clients. I was able to set my schedule, work when I wanted to, and even had more time for vacations. God gave me a promotion!" Karen said.

I asked Karen to make a list of what she learned from the hard times she experienced in the workplace. Here are her answers.

1. **You will come through it.** Remember, most problems are temporary.
2. **You will survive**. Even when you lose, there is life after loss.
3. **You will grow from your experiences.** Pain means gain.
4. **You will trust the Lord**. Remember, He has been faithful to you.
5. **You will get to know the Lord** in a deeper way because you have to depend on Him. Adversity takes you to a place of intimacy with Him.

Karen has also faced cancer. In 1982, she was in a sales meeting when she found out that she had melanoma cancer. Because of the adversity that she had been through in business, she knew that God was with her. He would walk her through it. The melanoma was classified as a stage 3 cancer. The doctors got it right before it went into the bloodstream. After surgery, her margins were free.

Whatever your place of difficulty is, God is there with you. Even when you are walking through the darkest nights, you are never alone. Call out to Him for help. He will move heaven to earth to guide you and be with you.

Planting in Others' Gardens

You can't plant in other gardens unless you set an example through your habits, what you represent, how you take hold of things, and how you live your life. Esther set this kind of standard.

Speaking to today's Christian working woman, you might be the only one in your place of business or office who is the living Bible. Esther was the spiritual leader of her palace—her workplace. She affected the people around her. Love was her banner.

So many people say that they don't have Christians working in their offices. These people might find that they are the ones that God has put there, just as Esther was placed. By your example, you may be able to reach someone for Christ or influence them greatly at the place where they are. For sure, everyone will be watching you. This is why it is so important to get your act together. Others are depending on you. They are waiting for you to come into maturity and get your house in order. Be that example, that mentor for Christ in the workplace. Esther will help you.

QUEEN ESTHER'S REFLECTION

Whether you are employed or not, you have a place of influence as a woman. Spend some time in prayer, asking God to show you what He would have you plant in others' lives in your place of influence.

Study Guide

1. What are the dangers of crossing a Haman in the workplace? How can we learn from Esther's plan?

2. What dangers in the workplace are you most susceptible to? Do you have a trusted friend who can share the load of these challenges through her friendship?

3. What are the daily practices that can strengthen your faith in the workplace?

4. List three people whose workplace behavior you admire and would like to emulate.

CHAPTER 11

Mordecai Mentors

Glimpses of Grace
"I have set watchmen on your walls, O Jerusalem."
—Isaiah 62:6

In 1980, I was attending a Bible study at my friend and mentor Eliza's home. Her husband, Dan, taught the lesson while Eliza hosted her guests afterwards with cake and coffee. One evening after the meeting was over, another friend, Pat, and I were helping Eliza tidy up. The two women were discussing a trip that was coming up. I did not know it then, but it would be God's timing for me.

"You need to take this trip!" Eliza told me with bold authority in her voice.

"Where?" I responded.

"Israel!" Eliza shot back.

"Israel? When?" I asked, not caring at all to go on a trip.

"In 30 days!" was Eliza's quick response.

"Thirty days," I laughed. "There is no way I can go to Israel in 30 days. I have two preteen age daughters and a business to run," I said confidently smiling back at both of them. There was no way I was going to go to Israel in a month. Then it came—the love bomb.

"Darling, when are you going to start praying and asking God what you should do, instead of saying no before you ask Him?" Eliza sweetly said to me.

Her words pierced my heart. I was a little stunned when Eliza said this. I knew she was right. I did need to pray more. I should pray about everything, but I did not feel that I should go to Israel and leave my daughters for 10 days. I went home and did as Eliza instructed. I prayed and asked God to show me without a doubt if this trip was of Him. My prayer went something like this:

"Lord, you know that Eliza is more advanced in prayer—but she has told me that I should ask You about everything. So, I am asking You to show me about this trip. Lord, make it really clear if I am to go, please. In the name of Jesus, I pray. Amen."

Amazingly the answer came soon. A client called and asked if I could go ahead and do all the design work on their project in two weeks! Then I could order everything while they were gone on a trip around the world. Amazingly, they were going to write me a check for the project and let me draw from the account while they were gone. That is almost unheard of. I felt that God was in the midst of it somehow.

A day or two later, another client requested almost the same situation. Then, my mother, who is a world traveler, phoned me to say that she had a strong desire to go to Israel!

She had exhausted her list of friends who traveled with her, and no one wanted to go to Israel at that time. I told her that Eliza had handed me the brochure and strongly suggested that I go on the trip. Mother moved on the opportunity to confirm what Eliza had stated.

Another part of this confirmation would be to have my daughters safely cared for. I am a very protective parent. The list of possible sitters was very short. It came down to one woman. Her name was Virginia. She was a *grandmotherly type*, a Christian, and knew us well. She had worked in my doctor's office at one point, so she was qualified to act quickly if need be.

I knew I was to go on this trip. But why, I did not know. I had an appointment in Jerusalem just as Esther had an appointment in the palace. My life was changed in an instant just like Esther's was when she won the heart of the king.

For some time, God had been speaking to me about forgiveness and marriage. At first, I did not want to hear anything about it because I had been so hurt by my first husband's abandonment of our family. As I became healed, I was open to all that God had for my life. It did not happen in an instant. The healing took place layer after layer. I was being restored and prepared for marriage to John.

John and I met on that trip to Israel. God confirmed that we should be together one morning in Jerusalem. The night before we had been in Bethlehem at Shepherd's Field, and afterwards our group went to the gift shop to purchase souvenir items for loved ones. It was there that a pastor in our group began a conversation with me. He said, "I see how you look when you are talking with John Platz."

Whoa! This man was in my private space. I immediately changed the subject. He laughed and said for me not to be embarrassed, that this was a good thing. Again I changed the subject. I knew that just the sight of John Platz made my heart flutter. It had been years since I had felt this kind of emotion. I was trying to control my inner feelings, but my heart was betraying me.

The next morning at breakfast, I noticed this same pastor getting up from his table. He was heading our way with a huge smile on his face. I knew that he was up to something. We were having breakfast with my mother and my friend Pat. Then it happened.

"God would not let me finish my meal. I am an evangelist, a pastor, and a prophet of God. He said for me to come over and speak these words over you: '*Not only are you an attractive couple, but God is putting you together as one in Him. There will be some rough edges, but He will take care of that.*'"

Just as God chose Esther's husband, He chose mine also. A short time later, John and I were married. I was being prepared without really knowing it. Everywhere I went, the discussions were on marriage. Trusting God to complete the plan for your life is the ultimate confidence we need have.

Esther accepted wise counsel. You cannot afford to have an I'm-right-and-they-are-wrong attitude or an I-am-not-bowing attitude in home situations. You must be open to see, hear, and be gently corrected. Wise counsel will always lead you to the right way of doing things.

Cultivating Spiritual Children

Mentoring is vital for personal growth. We all need to be mentored and to make a contribution by mentoring those who come after us. Mentors help us see beyond what we are capable of seeing. Having a plan is vital for mentoring, but just being there and caring for that person's needs is also important. The mentor can email, pray, and set an example, and this will cause the person mentored to be strengthened. You can help the other person set a higher standard than they see for themselves.

Mordecai showed that he was a consummate mentor in his relationship with Esther. He was committed to her well-being, and he made a daily investment in her life, even when she lived in the palace. He encouraged her to believe in herself, and when she needed a direct confrontation to see God's hand in her life, he was not afraid to deliver that confrontation, strongly. He walked with her through all the events in her life, and she knew she could trust him. He was her big-picture person.

The mentor Mordecai knew that God provides. He never doubted that God would provide deliverance for his people. He just wanted Esther to fulfill her role in the holy drama that was unfolding. He was truly a good mentor.

Mentoring is so needed in today's Christian community. The spiritually younger need the wisdom of the wiser, older, mature person. Mentoring is life-giving and life-changing. God created us to need each other. When you meet with someone on a regular basis, you invest in that person. As you do this, you continue to elevate and help them grow to a higher place. So many people get to a certain point and they feel *this is all that I can be* . . . . A mentor is placed in their lives to help them climb higher.

Cultivating a mentoring relationship can have an immense impact on both lives. For example, young Dwight L. Moody was working in his uncle's shoe shop when Mr. Kimball, a Sunday School teacher, visited him. Mr. Kimball felt the urge to share the love of Christ with the young man. Moody accepted Christ that day. Eventually, Moody became a great evangelist and publisher and began some wonderful Christian schools and a publishing company. The world has been blessed by what Dwight L. Moody did, and it is the result of one Sunday School teacher's visit.

Successful mentoring produces reproducers. Those who have been mentored become mentors. Mentors see the growth process when they mentor others. What you have imparted to them, they then give to others—grandchildren in the Lord!

Esther is an example of a "well mentored one" in Scripture. Mordecai recognized who she was spiritually. He answered the call to mentor her. He taught her, encouraged her, protected her, prayed for her, placed her, encouraged her, made a way for her, and brought her to the next level of impartation. He even stood guard at the gate watching. He was a full mentor to Esther. God entrusted Esther to Mordecai. And Mordecai knew what to do.

Grace Mothers

As I conduct seminars on the topic of spiritual transformation, I love to interact with those who attend. Hearing some of their stories, I have come to realize just how blessed I am to have been born into a family that is deeply rooted in faith and love, a family who also understands social, political, and divine protocol—the rules for living together in harmony and peace. Four beautiful women of grace, as different as night from day, were my "grace mothers." They modeled excellence for me—my mother, my two grandmothers, and Clara, our beloved family cook. Each, in her own area of expertise and with her own distinctive flavor, marked me forever.

As I matured I learned that I also needed to grow spiritually. For this purpose God sent other "grace mothers" who were not related by blood to mentor me in the deeper truths of gracious living and godliness. When I surrendered my will and accepted God's will, my life changed. God connected me with my mentors right away—anointed women of God. They came in rapid succession, each with their specialties.

- Eliza, my foundational mentor, taught me the power of knowing Scripture and the power of prayer.
- Mary, the gifting expert, called forth the prophetic voice in me. She prayed for my spiritual eyes to be opened and for me to receive a new level of discernment. She also alerted me to my other spiritual gifts and the anointing to do that work.
- Charlotte describes herself as the "mentoring nag." She "stayed on me," telling me that I was a writer. I almost missed that message.
- Last but not least, Doris called for the power gifts. She mentored me in deliverance, making sure that I knew what it was and how to use it when need be.

These women have the Esther anointing—"for such a time as this." They are purposed to make a difference in the world. They are strategically placed in position to pour into their spiritual daughters' lives. They, like Queen Esther, have an appointment to prepare the ones they mentor for their meeting with the King!

Today I mentor many spiritual daughters. They are easy for me to recognize. They stand out in a crowd. A mother can spot her daughters anywhere, and I look for them everywhere I go. When I see potential in a young woman, a love for God, and a heart to know more about Him, I know that I am to encourage and impart hope to her. As these women come under my wing for a season, I instruct each of them to read the Book of Esther in several translations. I want them to grasp the full meaning of a sacrificial calling such as hers. Esther was willing to trust God step-by-step—from the contest to her coronation day and beyond—not knowing which day might be her last.

Acting and Reacting

My friend's mother had a complete nervous breakdown. She was a genteel, sweet southern belle who had not been allowed to express strong feelings of any kind. She was reared by her two loving aunts and her mother. These women lived in denial. They did not want to shed any tears or hear any bad news.

Counselors will tell you that when you stuff anger down and do not allow it to come out, you will have problems. Your system may implode, and you are likely to have significant problems or a breakdown of some sort. Some researchers believe that many immune system diseases like rheumatoid arthritis, Crohn's disease, lupus, and others are a result of a person's way of living—not being able to let things out, but instead holding hurts and anger inside. The underlying message of this kind of oppression is hopelessness, extreme grief, and self-hatred.

Add to your library the book, *A More Excellent Way* by Henry W. Wright. This book details the spiritual roots of disease and provides pathways to wholeness. It is a must-read!

My friend Martha Wolfe has a master's degree in counseling. She shares this good word for mentors:

> When you are helping those who are hurting and the bottom is falling out for them, you can trust God to give you the word that He wants them to hear. Faithfully, God will give you revelation, a word of knowledge, a word of wisdom, a prophetic message, or a picture that He will allow you to interpret. He will advise you to listen to them talk. One of the main things you must do when a person comes in crisis is to be focused on what they say. The more desperate you are to hear Him, the more you will seek Him. I can tell you that every time I have asked for wisdom in counseling, He has given it.
>
> I will probably be the weirdest counselor you have ever been to, but when I get a blank mind, I know that I need to say: "God, where do we go from here? Give me a picture, vision, chapter in Scripture, or tell me what question to ask. Sometimes He tells me to tell the person to keep talking, or keep getting my directions, or I would go down rabbit trails.

Sometimes God gives me a picture at the beginning of the session then ties it together at the end of the session. When I meet with a person in crisis, I say, "I am so excited! God is getting ready to lead you to a whole new place." I speak hope into their lives. Usually the people are hurting and confused. They need someone to talk to—someone who will pray with them and encourage them.

Influencers

Every person has a God-given purpose. Your whole life is in pursuit of that purpose. We all have been given the ability to be people of influence—influencers for the Lord. We have a sphere of influence automatically built around us—our families, friends, and co-workers. We live our lives daily in front of them. What we do and say is a powerful way of communicating who we really are and what our standards are.

Our lives are meant to be connected to others. This is God's plan. This is why we need to be reconcilers, and not dividers. When you break relationship, you cut off the flow of influence coming and going into the other person's life. Opportunities and relationships will be stopped just as if a major artery has been cut off. This is not to say that the wrong, abusive relationships should not be stopped. The right relationships need to stay intact.

Where is your favor? Look around you. Who influences you? Whom do you influence? Do you have favor with man and woman? Favor with God? Take a new look at the honors God has bestowed upon you. Exercise your gifts. Pray for those people who have been given to you. Bless them. Instead of wanting to receive the blessing, become a blessing.

Use your influence for good.

Esther took her influence and used it for God's purposes. She did this even at the risk of losing her life. How often do we throw away a chance to be great for God? Too often, I'm sure. Why do we stop right at the point where the discipline starts taking place? Probably because it starts to get hard right about then. The enemy comes in to steal and destroy whatever God has put in place. He is the disrupter. Sadly, if we just went a little longer, trusted God more, we would have conquered whatever stood in the way! Take a good look at what holds you back from your place of influence.

QUEEN ESTHER'S REFLECTION

Mordecai, as a mentor, was possibly the most important person in Esther's life. He pointed clearly to God's purpose for her at a time of crucial decision making for Esther. Imagine for a moment the result if he had neglected her, or if she had ignored his challenge. Do you still think a mentor is a "nice extra" in life?

Study Guide

1. List five people who have given you guidance at a crucial time in your life. These are your mentors.

2. Do you currently have a relationship with a strong mentor? Make time to cultivate that blessing for yourself.

3. List three people you know who could benefit from your knowledge and experience as a Christian woman. These are people for whom you could be a mentor.

4. Most Christian women don't recognize their own mentoring skills because of a misplaced sense of humility. Many women also are reluctant to ask someone to mentor them because they feel it will be an imposition. What ideas do you have for overcoming these barriers so that you are mentoring and being mentored regularly in your life?

CHAPTER 12

Enlarging Your Borders

Glimpses of Grace
"And they blessed Rebekah and said to her:
'Our sister, may you become the mother of thousands of
ten thousands.'"
—Genesis 24:60

ECOME A blessing! Be a blessing. Forget receiving a blessing!" I can hear Esther teaching us. Esther would tell us over and over not to be apprehensive. She would say get rid of the old, the past, the things that weigh you down. I can hear Esther's words of wisdom: "Stop taking from everybody. Start doing, giving, and praying for others. Do not constantly hold your hand out for *your* blessing."

I can hear Esther again saying: "Change your ways, stop

sitting and desiring to be fed. Get up! Move forward. Be proactive as a blessing to others!"

A natural by-product of growing and maturing is enlarging one's borders. The more you live, the more areas you grow to have mastered. The more success, the more territory you have, natural and spiritual. Esther certainly lived this. Esther enlarged her borders as she enlarged her sphere of influence. God's name is never mentioned in her story, but is visible in every situation and step of Esther's journey.

Esther received and accepted the enlarging of her borders in faith. God's plan for her was high visibility, larger places to receive people, open waters of opportunity, destruction of boundaries, open palace doors, and finally a life as queen, close to the king's heart.

Enlarging Her Borders

When Esther became the most powerful woman in the world, her influence expanded with her. Not only did she have the ear of the king and the favor of God, but she had the respect of her people. With those things in place, her ability to do great things was at a pinnacle. Position prepares one for power. If used correctly, privilege can be a mighty tool to do many good things. This is what prominent people know. The world opens up for them. When we are able to use our influence for things that are dear to God's heart, we become conduits of blessings to others.

How do we take new territory? Start with being bold with your faith. Because God has more for you than you imagine, whatever you are seeing right now is clearly not the big picture. Life is larger than what we are feeling and experiencing. I can remember times when I felt nothing but failure—failed marriage, failed financially, failed educationally. Those were temporary emotions. They were not based on what God was going to do with my life. It is difficult to see the blessing when you are hurting. All these feelings that I had were temporary. They were based on past performance, not my future!

As I began to grow in my walk with the Lord, my past became just that. I reached for new territory—the plans and purposes of God. He had new friends, a new church, and new dreams for me.

You do not know what is ahead. Every day is a new beginning. That is why when you go to sleep, thank God for the day past and thank Him for the new one tomorrow.

New Territory

My ministry has taken me to some very interesting places. One Christmas I was invited to do a signing for my book, *Social Graces,* at the annual Festival of Trees in Atlanta, a very popular Christmas event. As an interior designer, I usually do something to help make the event beautiful and festive. This year my involvement was to meet and greet some of the festivalgoers.

John and I arrived early and set our books out for the talk that I would give. Noticing that most everyone was gathered over into the corner of the facility, I asked what was going on. "Oh, that's Chipper Jones. He's signing baseballs," someone said.

Hmm. I wonder how long he is going to be here? I thought.

This went on for the hour that I was to sign my new books.

Then with a few minutes left, a man walked by John, and they began talking. I was intrigued. This man did not look like anyone who would be interested in my book or the etiquette and manners part of it. He was a man's man. John kept pointing over to me and the stack of books in front of me. Soon, the man walked over to speak to me. I was convinced that John had asked him to do this. But then out of his mouth came: "Would you mind staying a few minutes longer? I have a group of young people who need to hear what you have to say!"

"Certainly. I would be glad to do that," I found myself saying. Really, I was delighted.

The man identified himself as the head of the local Division of Family and Child Services (DFCS). I would be speaking with 40 children from foster homes and other situations in which their parents could not take care of them.

The kids, aged 15 to18, came strolling in and took their places. Most of them looked unkempt and sort of ragtag. Fashion has certainly changed since I was in high school!

Staring these youngsters in the face, I suddenly wished that I was cool! I am cool about some things, but I do not see myself as kid cool! I knew that I had about 12 minutes with them, and I wanted to impart some message of grace to them—my Esther school of protocol!

"The moment someone meets you, they will form an opinion of you within the first two seconds," I said to 80 eyes staring at me!

The most incredible thing happened. Amazingly, they sat up, closed their legs, took off their hats and looked straight at me! They were perfect angels looking for the next assignment. It startled me!

Then for the next 15 or so minutes I told them four things—how to stand and hold yourself in a positive way; how to give eye-to-eye contact; how to give a proper handshake; and last, but certainly not least, how to thank the person who has hosted you!

Time flew by! I gave each one of them a copy of the book. They were off that day with a crash course in manners . . . and a book they promised to read. It was fun! Not long after this event, I was invited to do this for a larger group from DFCS. Seems that word of my talk had gotten around.

This time I was prepared. I enlisted some of the kids to role-play with me. This was fun as they acted out how NOT to get a job and many more comical situations. Then another group role-played the right way to do an interview and GET the job!

God had enlarged my territory. I was interacting with younger people—a group I would not have chosen, simply because I did not think they could relate to me. I was wrong. God had prepared the way and granted me royal favor.

The Land of Pure Grace

Several months later, I received a phone call from a woman I did not know. She introduced herself as Lorraine. She complimented me on my ability to relate to young people. I assumed that she was a part of the DFCS program. She asked if I was available to speak to "some little girls in trouble."

"Oh, yes! I would be able to do that," I replied, not knowing where or who these girls were. I requested that she send the date, time, and address to my office. The speaking engagement was two months away.

A few days before this event, my daughter Margo asked if I would go with her to check on the event she was working on at the Atlanta History Center. It coincided with my speaking date. I said sure, if she would go with me afterwards to speak to the girls in trouble. We set that as a date.

Margo is my youngest daughter. She is 36 years old, but looks much younger. She looks a lot like Britney Spears. She is precious, loving, tenderhearted, and a joy to all who know her. She is a very talented interior designer. She also does not promote herself. She waits for God to move her forward. I love her dearly.

On the morning of the two events, I made a quick appearance on television to promote the Atlanta Symphony Decorator's Show House. I was dressed in a pale pink knit suit—pink looks pretty on television. I usually wear a trademark silk flower or pin. This day I was wearing a large, white, French silk peony. When I left the television studio, I thought for a moment about what I was wearing. It seemed fine for speaking to some girls in trouble. At least it seemed that way then.

After going with Margo to check out her event, she and I traveled to my meeting. I mentioned to her that I might want her to say a little something to encourage the girls since she was closer to their age. She let me know that she would think about it and get back to me. Like most mothers and daughters, we talked and really didn't pay too much attention to anything else. Then Margo said, "Mom, where are we going?"

I looked up and there was a huge roll of barbed wire on top of the chain-link fence.

"Hmmm! I'm not sure!"

"I am! This looks like a prison!" Margo said with excitement in her voice.

"Hmmm, I guess so!"

"Mom, did you know that we were going to a prison?" Margo said, looking a little disgusted that I was unaware of where I was going.

"Not really. I knew that there were some little girls in trouble, but . . ."

"How much trouble are these girls in!?" Margo shot back.

We drove in the confined area, parked the car, and walked up the sidewalk that led to the secured entrance to the facility. Margo poked me in the back and said, "I've decided that I am not going to do any of the talking, so don't call on me to speak, OK?"

"Hmm, OK." I said, more concerned about where I was going than what she said.

Lorraine, the chaplain, greeted us in the reception area. She told us how happy the girls were that we were coming to speak. We signed in. I suddenly took notice of my pink outfit and my double stand of pearls. Yikes . . . this is *not* what I would choose to wear to speak here. Well, it's too late to change now! Margo had on hot pink jeans and a starched white top. She looked like the perfect daughter!

Margo and I followed an armed guard. We walked through several huge metal lockdown doors, and finally entered a large activities room that was also a basketball court. There were probably 100 boys over to the right and maybe 25 girls lined up to the left. They were dressed in blue prison garb with orange flip-flops. These were the meanest-looking girls I had ever seen—not my usual social graces girls. Upon the sight of these girls, Margo poked me again and reminded me that she was not going to speak.

I could see that the girls were not happy. Well, that's an understatement. They were whining and making gestures that they didn't want to go to chapel. As we got closer to them, I could hear them saying things like: "Who is that woman? I hate her. I don't want to hear anything that she has to say . . . .Please, don't make us go! And who is that with her? We hate her too!"

Sergeant Brown, the armed six-foot female guard, had a billy club in her hand. She yelled at them to line up and move forward. None of them wanted to go into the room for an hour's chapel time—as a matter of fact, I didn't want to go either. Then the sergeant said, "It's either chapel or lockdown!" That seemed to move them forward. Margo told me later that she thought they were considering lockdown over hearing me say anything!

Then it began. What happened next was straight out of a movie! The girls were restless. They hated me. They were hissing at me, rolling their eye towards the ceiling. Some were banging their heads on the little desks where they were sitting. Most were very defiant-looking and really scary to me. They were very vocal that they did not want to be there. It was a very tense room.

By this time Margo had told me at least five times not to call on her to say anything. She took a seat behind me at the teacher's desk. She was confident that she was out of the picture and that I was meeting one of my life's greatest speaking challenges!

Usually not at a loss for words, I was silently begging God to get me out of there. Then Lorraine introduced me as an interior designer. They almost bolted out of their chairs. They were sure then that they hated me. I came forward and began to talk. It was pitiful. I looked at my watch. I had 55 minutes left. They were so distracting that I could not concentrate. The room was filled with demonic activity. I knew it. I had no idea how this was going to turn out.

I told the Lord, "If you will get me through this, I will always read beyond the second paragraph. I will *know* where I am going to speak. HELP! 911!"

Then it happened. I laughed and said, "I have never been before such a rude group of people. I am at a loss as what to say to you." As soon as that sentence was out of my mouth, I began to laugh hysterically. I could not stop. Something broke in the spiritual realm. *God had shown up!* Joy was in the house! I was anointed to do what I was there to do. Inside I felt like Wonder Woman! I howled and asked them questions at the same time. They thought that I had gone crazy and were happy about that! They were finally behaving, or at least still, for a moment.

It was a hilarious scene. I asked them to tell me the one thing that each had that was special about them. As I pointed to them individually, they responded. The first girl said that she wrote poetry. I was shocked. The second said that she liked to do hair. It went all the way around the room. It was working! All along I was laughing that crazy laugh!

I felt such a sense of power that I said, "You are going to receive so much truth today that you will hug me when I leave!"

One girl said, "You ain't touching me!"

Another girl said, "I ain't hugging you, and you ain't touching me!"

I thought: *Lord, I must have lost my mind. I was so excited that "You will want to hug me when you leave" just flew out of my mouth! I am afraid of them! I have no intention of touching any of them!*

Anyway, I continued laughing and asking each a question until I felt the "power anointing" beginning to wear off. Sort of like when the Novocain wears off at the dentist's office. Then is when I heard the Lord say, "Margo has the message! Call her forward!"

Yikes! I thought. *She will kill me! She told me over and over not to include her in any of this. Margo is so tender, I just cannot do this to her.* Then I came to my senses. God had planned for her to have the central message. I was her warm-up act.

I didn't bother to look around to see what Margo's reaction was when I announced that she had the message for them that afternoon. She did bump into me as she passed by. I knew what that meant . . . *traitor mother . . . I will get you for this.* I knew I would rather deal with her than with God for being disobedient.

Margo stepped forward and sat on the corner of the desk. Here's how she tells the story.

I was scared to death standing up there thinking that this would be my toughest audience to date! I was going to get even with Mom. I told her at least five times *not to call on me to speak*! What was she thinking? What in the world will I talk about? I cannot relate to these rude, awful girls. What do we have in common?

Just at that moment, it hit me. We look very different, come from different places, families, cultures, but the pain is still the same. I thanked the Lord for giving me that pearl of wisdom. I shared with the girls. They were completely still. They took in every word. You could have heard a pin drop!

God really showed up in those 20 minutes. It seemed like hours as I shared with them the hurt and pain that I experienced in my divorce. My message was that though we look different, the pain is the same. No one hurts less because they are financially better off, or have more family support—pain is pain. At that moment I bonded with those girls—sister to sister, friend to friend, mentor to mentored. I felt the connection.

I told them that until I took responsibility for my part in the end of my marriage, God could not release me into another healthy relationship. I would just go from one failed relationship to another in a cycle of the same action and the same results—always being the victim and never being responsible for all the things that I did to make the relationship a failure.

A light went on in the girls. I could see it in their eyes. I told them how important it is to have respect for yourself, to get self-confidence, and to set boundaries. It is OK to say no and mean no!

When my time was up, they all clapped for me. Sergeant Brown raised her billy club up in the air and yelled out, "Line up to hug Mrs. Platz!"

They did what the sergeant said do. Each girl got in line, eager to hug Mom! It was amazing. After they hugged her, they walked over to me and thanked me and hugged me. It was very emotional to see these troubled girls accept us and receive what we had said. It touched my life and changed my opinion of situations like this. I saw the miracle— they went from hate to love!

One of the girls asked me if she could talk with me. She told me her very sad story of having a baby at 12 years of age, and that this had caused her mother to insist that she give the baby up for adoption. Her boyfriend was furious. The girl was so desperate for the approval of her boyfriend that she tried to kill her mother!

After telling me this sad story, the girl looked at me and asked me how to get self-confidence. It almost broke my heart. She was so young and in so much trouble. I was playing with Barbie dolls when I was 12! Then she told me that she wanted to be just like me. I told her to take a few steps each day—and to try to forgive her mother, her boyfriend, and herself.

After we hugged the last girl, Sergeant Brown walked us to the secured area. I heard her tell my mother, "You are some kind of woman! I watched you get those girls' attention. Not many folks can calm that group!"

I had to laugh because Mom was a real comedian that day, not her usual southern elegant style of speaking. Sergeant Brown led us into the courtyard and toward our car. Then we heard a tapping noise from across the courtyard—a tap, tap, tapping sound. I turned around and reported to Mom that the girls were tapping on the window to get our attention. They were waving at us.

Wow! What a day. I will never forget the platform that the Lord gave us. I believe that we were sent in to do a deep work for the Lord with those girls. I do not know who was blessed the most!

The Irresistible Fragrance of a Godly Woman

Esther's fragrance was powerful. Her fragrance lured the most powerful man of that day. Like many women of the Bible, Esther was a feminine force for God. We are meant to be noticed by the aroma of Christ. We should be able to be spotted and noticed by those who have spiritual eyes to see. God will place you right in the middle of the world where He intends to use you. It is there that your fragrance will come forth. It will accomplish what it is intended to do.

Below I have listed the women of the Bible whom I admire. Each has a fragrance that is powerful. These women changed the world. Each has a story. Each had an intimate relationship with God.

Queen Esther: a Jewish woman of great beauty, grace, and favor went through a lot of discipline to prepare herself for her audience with the king. She saved her people's lives. She is known for the famous statement Mordecai made of her, that God brought her to her position as queen "*for such a time as this.*" Her fragrance was courage, which saved the nation of Israel.

Sarah, the wife of Abraham: received by faith the word that she would be the mother of many nations. She gave birth at 90 years of age. Her son Isaac begat Jacob who begat Benjamin whose lineage begat Esther—and the story goes on. Her fragrance was faith.

Hannah, a prayerful mother: dedicated her son, Samuel, for God's use and glory. Hannah was a mighty woman of prayer and persistence. Hannah prayed. Her prayers impacted an entire nation, leaving a legacy through her son. Her fragrance was humility.

Deborah, the prophetess: sat on the outskirts of the city as a judge to dispense wisdom to the leaders of that day. Deborah was a leader. Her office was one of the first *rooms to go*! It was a portable desk placed under a palm tree. She led her nation from this vantage point with godly wisdom, advising General Barak with strategic battle plans. Her fragrance was strength.

Ruth, a woman of great loyalty: possessed obedience and faith. Widowed at an early age, Ruth did not to abandon her mother-in-law, Naomi. Ruth trusted that God would provide for her. She was committed to doing the right thing. The Lord redeemed her life and provided her with another husband, Boaz. Her fragrance was loyalty.

The Proverbs 31 woman of excellence: a godly example of womanhood. Known as *Mrs. Far Above Rubies*, this woman had her priorities right. She saw to the needs of her household. She was a woman of provision, constantly buying and selling linen and properties! Her fragrance was excellence.

Mary, the mother of Jesus: a young teenage mother who cradled the Messiah. Mary had the most influence over Jesus as His mother. Her fragrance was the pure love of a mother.

Elizabeth, the mother of John the Baptist and cousin of Mary: foretold the birth of Jesus. She prophesied that

Jesus's ministry would be greater than that of her son, John the Baptist. Her fragrance was truth.

Anna, the prophetess: wanted to live just to see the Messiah before she died. She lived to see Mary and Joseph bring the baby Jesus to the Temple. Anna had spiritual eyes to see. She recognized Jesus. Her fragrance was godly wisdom.

Mary Magdalene, one of the women who followed Jesus: the first evangelist to go and tell that Jesus was no longer in the grave. He had risen! Her fragrance was a zest and zeal that evangelized the world.

Mary and Martha, the hospitality duo: loved and served the Lord. Mary was at His feet while Martha was busy in the kitchen. Jesus told Martha to look at Mary's example of devotion to Him. Their fragrance was serving through love and devotion.

The Woman at the well: the wife of more than one husband and living in sin when she met Jesus and was forgiven. Her fragrance was gratefulness.

Lydia, the wealthy businesswoman: a seller of purple. After she and her household were baptized, she begged Paul to be a guest in her house. She financially underwrote Paul and Silas's ministry. She opened her home for hospitality for these first-century apostles. Her fragrance was wealth and influence!

Priscilla, wife of Aquila: helped advance Paul's ministry by opening their home for ministry. They were Jewish tentmakers. While Paul was in Corinth, the couple provided him with lodging. Paul taught them the things of God. Later they helped spread the gospel to others. Her fragrance was hospitality.

You! What will be written about you? What will be your fragrance?

Each woman modeled character, faith, and integrity. Each had a divine destiny. They were female leaders and role models—world changers. All were very clear as to their purpose. These women were ordinary people, just like you and me. Their lives reflected their love for God. They were God's women, placed where He could use them. They had influence because God granted them favor.

Our Opportunity

Esther's Palace! What an address! What a place of opportunity for ministry! This woman was certainly an example to follow for those who love God. We know her story. How do we take her model of excellence and execute the things that God has for us to do?

Once one leaves the palace grounds, what's next? What are the opportunities for today's Esthers? Our challenge and ministry opportunities are often away from home and out in the world. They are every place we go and to every person we meet. We are to go into *all the world* to be examples of people of faith.

Because Esther was a faithful, focused, favored woman of God, she was able to affect the world. The results of her obedience and courage took her beyond the palace grounds and outside the court. Her obedience to protect her people caused a great change of plans. The enemy had targeted the Jews for destruction, but God had other plans for them. There is so much for us to learn from Esther. Her life should be a study for all to seek wisdom and apply to their lives.

QUEEN ESTHER'S REFLECTION

Lord, expand my faith. Give me the courage that I need in this hour. Lord, grant me the ability to love more, do more, and be more for Your purposes. Enlarge my heart to receive more of You!

Study Guide

1. Do a word study on *faith*.

2. How many times have you been called to love more?

3. Name three instances when you cried out to God for help!

4. How has God expanded your borders?

5. Who has encouraged you to grow in your faith?

6. Make a hope list for the Lord. Ask for help!

CHAPTER 13

Esther's Legacy of Grace

Glimpses of Grace
*"For it is God who works in you both to will and to do
for His good pleasure."*
—Philippians 13:2

ESTHER'S LEGACY remains today. The fruit of her sacrificial life lives on in Israel and through all who read about her in the Book of Esther. Regally, she stands in God's Hall of Fame as a bold woman of faith. She shares this honor with Ruth as one of two women with Old Testament books named after them. Esther, royal mother of Israel, is revered today as her story is told in Christian churches and Jewish synagogues alike.

Esther is known for having a heart for things that God had a heart for. When she took her palace position and lined it up with her holy heart for God, she brought forth the greatest gift of sacrifice and saved a nation. She did not fear death, and she embraced her destiny!

Esther gladly used her gifts for the Lord. She took what was bestowed upon her and offered it back to the Lord. Her holy heart didn't fear anything. She took everything that God had allowed her to have—favor, royal robes, oils, perfumes—and allowed it to be a broken, anointed vessel. She poured oil on the sacrifices and risked it all with indelible words when she said, "If I perish, I perish!"

Great Is His faithfulness

God is faithful; this is true. He has been so faithful to me. I would be lost and hopeless without Him. I owe Him every honor and give Him all praise. Thank You, Lord, for all that You have done in my life. Your faithfulness to me is so great. I love You. I cannot imagine a day without You. I cannot imagine my life without You.

I often remind others of the faithfulness of God. When you need to be encouraged, ask God to do this for you. He will. I have often asked for this and received a phone call or email that had just the right encouragement for the day. I call these kisses from God.

What you do today will set in place the blessings that will come down to your children. God loves to bless the generations. You may be savoring some blessing because you had godly parents or grandparents. What you do today spiritually will provide for your children and their children!

God delivered Esther as an orphan being raised by her older cousin. She had a small chance of having any kind of life. God delivered her from obscurity into the palace. The Lord gave her favor, and she became queen instead of a concubine.

A Mighty Move of God

One of the great benefits of being asked to speak in churches is the opportunity to meet many dynamic women of faith. I can see the wisdom of Esther blooming boldly in so many of these women today. Chrissie Shaheen is one of these women. Her ministry, His Palace Ministry, focuses on reconciling us to God and us to one another. Her ministry has been headquartered in Israel since 1998.

Chrissie's family is of Arabic descent, and they are Christians. The Shaheen family was one of five families who established the Christian Arab community of Ramallah, Israel, in the early 1500s. They came from Jordan where they were running from a sheik who had threatened their lives. In the late 1930s her grandparents moved to America and bore their first born son, Chrissie's father. Chrissie's father married a southern belle from Dalton, Georgia, a blonde-haired, blue-eyed, pink-skinned beauty.

At 15 years of age, Chrissie had an opportunity to go to Ramallah but had no desire to do so. However, while going through a divorce years later, she decided to accept the offer of a friend to go to Israel. It was on that tour that she met two Bible teachers who lived in the Dalton area. As she walked the land of Israel, she met Jesus at every site. She met believers who did not hold back in sharing their love for Jesus. It was a spiritual awakening that impacted her deeply. She came home and for two years she attended their Bible study.

Israel plays a part in God's kingdom purposes today. Jesus is coming back to Israel. He loves Israel. Chrissie met a different aspect of Him at these Bible studies and began falling in love with Jesus through this focus on Israel. She developed a deeper relationship with Jesus Christ. She returned to Israel with the Bible teachers in 1998. At that time a piece of her heart stayed in Jerusalem. She went back to Dalton, weeping and asking the Lord to allow her to serve Him in Jerusalem, even if it only for three months. That would be the desire of her heart!

God answered that prayer. The Lord cleared her schedule for her to go to the Jerusalem House of Prayer for All Nations. She was able to join people from 200 nations who gather every year in Jerusalem to pray. From there everything got started—her three months in Jerusalem became six months. She and some of her friends started ministering to people on the streets in the Christian-Arab communities.

"There is a tiny Christian Arabic Church with 60 members, all under the age of 30. They meet every day of the week to pray and to seek God. The church is in the Old City of Jerusalem behind a door on one of the narrow stone streets. No one would know that it was there. Behind the door you find a courtyard and a stone pathway. You walk up a tiny staircase to the sanctuary. The church is built with big ivory stones aptly called Jerusalem stones. The ceiling is dome-shaped and the stone on the floor is called Jerusalem bloodstone because it has a red vein running through it.

"The passion of the parishioners' hearts is to worship God and pray. All they want is God. It is so powerful. A lot of those young people are now in ministry themselves.

Many are a part of a relief ministry going into the West Bank and sharing the gospel with Muslims. They want people to know Jesus. There are about 150 new converts to Christ from those people who went out to evangelize," Chrissie shared.

Starting in 1998, Chrissie began to build relationships with the Christian Arabs and Messianic Jewish believers through meetings of reconciliation. She did not know what that would entail, but eventually she began to see changes. She came to have the following understanding of true reconciliation:

1. First, there must be reconciliation to the Lord—after salvation, a transformation of our hearts in knowing we are a child of God and ultimately the bride of Christ.

2. Second, there must be reconciliation with our enemies—the world will know Him by the love we have for one another.

3. Third, since everything began in Jerusalem and will end in Jerusalem, then it is critical for Christian Arabs and Messianic Jews to show the love of Christ with love for one another. Only Jesus can reconcile people who hated each other for thousands of years. Step 2 cannot happen until step 1 is in process.

The history of the Christian Arab Church is extensive. It is a combination of Roman Catholic, Greek Orthodox, the Protestant Church, the Evangelical Church, and the Muslim Background Believers (MBB). Most of the women Chrissie works with are the MBB or Evangelical Christian Arabs who have come from a Greek Orthodox or Catholic background.

Chrissie shares, "Most of our Messianic Jewish sisters are Israeli and some as old as 20 years in the faith. They have come from secular families whose Jewish identity is tied to their nationality. Many of them are children of Holocaust survivors. If this great divide is to be bridged, then much healing and restoration in our relationship with God must occur. You must reframe your mind and believe in your heart that you are a child of God and the bride of Christ."

Talk about setting a table in the presence of your enemies—wow! I am always amazed when I read this in Psalm 23. When you are hurt by someone, you do not really want to be in their company—and especially break bread with them! This is true about the long estrangement between Christian Arabs and the Israeli Messianic Jews. They do not trust each other, but they are in the family of believers and desire to know one another. However, they are cautious in doing so. Chrissie sees the need to bring these two factions together in unity. She has designed the most wonderful way of doing this—at retreat spas and banquets! Esther would approve! Here are some of the things Chrissie is doing.

Dead Sea Spa Day: Chrissie understands the Esther beauty anointing. We need full inner and outer healing. This is so critical to be whole and effective. We need to remove the deep stuff from our past—hurts, sins, and even rigid religious spirits. One of the first retreats she planned was a spa time at the Dead Sea. Imparting some of His truths outwardly, she invited women to join her for a time of healing and restoration.

Driving out of Jerusalem about 45 minutes, Christian Arabic women who are busy working in ministry put their cares away and allowed God to love them. Mud packs, massage therapy, manicures, oil rubs, and delicious meals gave these hardworking women great pleasure and relaxation. Chrissie asked them to throw their cares off and toss them in the Dead Sea. Only the things that God wanted to resurrect would be resurrected.

Esther's Bridal Preparation Weekend: Chrissie organized a delightful Esther weekend at a convent in a suburb of Jerusalem. The invitation read: "*Please come to the rehearsal of the Wedding Supper of the Lamb!*" Who would refuse that offer?

Chrissie provided a sumptuous banquet—fruits, flowers, breads, meats, and specialties of the area. The guests were a mixed international group: Messianic Jews, Christian Arabs, and internationals. All these women came for time with the Lord and one another. Much focus was placed on worship, prayer, and restoring our identity as the bride of Christ. Special treats like massage, hair styling, manicures, and pedicures were also part of the package. The nun in charge and the location are like none other.

"Sister Catherine, the overseer of the facility, is an amazing believer. She broke my mind-set of what a nun is. She is a precious, contemporary woman. I love that she dances before the Lord. She has a heart for reconciliation and makes it possible through this facility that can house 50 people for such events. She and her staff of 8, who live and work at the convent, prepare wonderful meals for their guests and treat them with the finest hospitality," Chrissie said.

The convent is located where the ark of the covenant rested for 40 years until King David brought it back into Jerusalem. Wow! God's presence is still there today. The sisters let Chrissie decorate the rooms as she wanted to and even gave her the use of the nuns' private chapel to host the meetings. The message for the event was it's OK to be beautiful! Throughout the weekend worship, inner healing and special prayer took place.

Reconciliation Retreat: Another wonderful retreat Chrissie organized took place about two hours from Jerusalem at the Sea of Galilee. This is one of my favorite spots on earth. John and I have been there twice. This birthplace of Mary Magdalene is now the location of a wonderful Christian retreat center. This retreat is devoted to worship.

For the Reconciliation Retreat, Chrissie used Exodus 24, the story of Moses going to the top of the mountain to meet with God and experience His embrace. A group of 33 believers—Christian Arabs, Muslim Background Believers, Messianic Jews, and various international believers—worshipped in all three languages: Hebrew, Arabic, and English! God broke the wall of separation and the women started washing each other's feet and reconciling their past hurts. Arabs and Jews ministered to one another, Germans and Jews reconciled over the Holocaust, and even individual conflicts were resolved. God did a mighty work that weekend. It was emotional, delightful, joyful, and fun—yet difficult too.

Esthers of Today

You can be an Esther of today—are you prepared? These are women of serious prayer and fasting. They are devoted to the causes of the Lord—what He loves and what He desires us to love. These precious saints are committed to go and serve, love at a moment's notice, and are available to be mothers in Israel whenever needed. They are downsizing, moving, parting with more possessions, preparing to be unencumbered so as to move at a moment's notice.

Esther used her beauty and wisdom as an ultimate sacrifice, the embodiment of the best of the best. Courageous, she was an empty vessel. God placed her in the right place at the right time. She was to save her people from ultimate demise. Beauty, timing, grace, humility, love—it was all about love, sacrificial love!

Esther—*royal and exquisite—grand and noble, spiritually beautiful.*

QUEEN ESTHER'S REFLECTION

Father, as You gave Esther to us as a grace model of a truly beautiful woman, may each of us take from her what we need to be spiritually beautiful. Help us see far beyond the outer beauty and palace trappings. Allow us the privilege to know her, understand her, and be her in this age.

Study Guide

1. What is the highest calling that God has purposed only you to do?

2. What have you learned from Esther's life that you want to apply to your life?

3. With what part of Esther's legacy has God specifically gifted you?

4. How will what you do today influence the generations that follow?

5. How has God made you spiritually beautiful? How are you using that for Him?

Appendix

"For Zion's sake I will not hold My peace,
And for Jerusalem's sake I will not rest,
Until the righteousness goes forth as a brightness,
And her salvation as a lamp that burns.
The Gentiles shall see your righteousness,
And all the kings your glory.
You shall be called by a new name,
Which the mouth of the Lord will name.
You shall also be a crown of glory
In the hand of the Lord,
And a royal diadem
In the hand of your God."
—Isaiah 62:1–3

The Sinner's Prayer

If you have never prayed the prayer of salvation, here it is.

To be born again, you must ask God for forgiveness, confess with your mouth that Jesus is Lord, and invite Jesus to be your Lord and Savior.

Please pray this prayer and invite the Lord Jesus Christ into your life. And when you do this, you have made your reservation for the marriage supper of the Lamb, which will take place in heaven.

Heavenly Father,
I come to You in prayer asking for the forgiveness of my sins.
I confess with my mouth and believe with my heart that Jesus
Christ is Your Son, and that He died on the Cross at Calvary
that I might be forgiven of my sins, and that I will have eternal
life in the kingdom of heaven.

Father, I believe that Jesus was born of a virgin, died, and rose
from the dead. He now sits at Your right hand. I ask You right
now, Lord Jesus, to come into my life and be my personal Lord
and my Savior.

I repent of my sins. I ask You, Lord Jesus, to wash me clean and make me whole. I ask You to make me new, whole, and cleansed from all wrong.

I will worship You all the days of my life!

Because Your Word is truth, I confess with my mouth that I am born again in You and cleansed by the blood of Jesus!

In the name of Jesus Christ, I pray.
Amen.

Welcome to the family of God!

New Hope® Publishers is a division of WMU®, an international organization that challenges Christian believers to understand and be radically involved in God's mission. For more information about WMU, go to www.wmu.com. More information about New Hope books may be found at www.newhopepublishers.com. New Hope books may be purchased at your local bookstore.

You may enjoy

The Best Is Yet to Come
*Designing Your Future
with Style*
Ann Platz
ISBN 1-56309-912-8

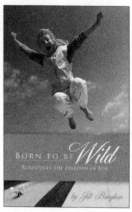

Born to Be Wild
Rediscover the Freedom of Fun
Jill Baughan
ISBN 10 1-59669-048-8
ISBN 13 978-1-59669-048-6

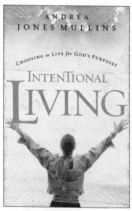

Intentional Living
*Choosing to Live
for God's Purposes*
Andrea Jones Mullins
ISBN 1-56309-927-6

Available in bookstores everywhere

For information about these books
or any New Hope product, visit
www.newhopepublishers.com.